ZEPPELIN

ZEPPELIN

The Story of the Zeppelin Airships

Hans G. Knäusel

Translated from the German by David Johnston

Schiffer Publishing Ltd
4880 Lower Valley Road • Atglen, PA 19310

Photo Credits

Dornier GmbH: 23

Luftschiffbau Zeppelin GmbH (Zeppelin Museum Friedrichshafen): 9, 10 (1), 11 (2), 14, 17, 18 (1), 21, 23, 30, 37, 38 (2), 39, 40, 41, 44 (2), 45 (2), 46, 47, 48 (1), 50, 51, 54 (2), 55 (1), 58 (3), 59, 60 (2), 61 (3), 62 (1), 63 (2), 65, 69, 72 (2), 73, 77 (1), 78, 80, 81, 82 (1), 84 (2), 87 (1), 88 (2), 89 (1), 90, 91 (2), 94 (3), 96, 97 (2), 98 (1), 100, 102 (3), 103, 104, 106 (2), 108, 109 (2), 110, 111 (2), 112 (3), 113, 114 (4), 115 (2), 116 (2), 117 (1), 126 (1), 137, 139, 142 (2), 145 (2), 147.

Gütschow Collection: 55 (2), 68, 95 (1).

Knäusel Collection: 10 (1), 19, 22, 27, 36, 48 (1), 49, 58 (1), 60 (1), 62 (1), 66 (2), 67, 68, 74 (2), 77 (1), 82 (3), 84 (1), 85, 86, 87 (1), 88 (3), 89 (1), 92, 93, 94 (1), 95 (1), 97 (1), 98 (2), 106 (1), 112 (1), 115 (1), 116 (2), 117 (1), 118, 119 (2), 121, 122, 123 (2), 124 (2), 126 (2), 135, 136, 143 (2), 144, 146 (2).

Zahnradfabrik Friedrichshafen AG: 8, 18 (1), 24.

Zeppelin Luftschifftechnik AG: 129 (1), 130 (2), 131 (2), 132 (2).

Library of Congress Control Number: 2013940667

This book is a combination of works originally published in German under the series title
Zepplelin Die Geschichte der Zeppelin-Luftschiffe
Konstrukteure-Technik-Unternehmen

Printed in China.
ISBN: 978-0-7643-4478-7

We are interested in hearing from authors with book ideas on related topics.

Published by Schiffer Publishing Ltd.
4880 Lower Valley Road
Atglen, PA 19310
Phone: (610) 593-1777
FAX: (610) 593-2002
E-mail: Info@schifferbooks.com.
Visit our web site at: www.schifferbooks.com
Please write for a free catalog.
This book may be purchased from the publisher.
Try your bookstore first.

Contents

Foreword

This book is a revised and expanded version of *Der Zeppelin Luftschiffbau im Spiegel der Fachliterature*, H.G. Knäusel's contribution to *Leichter als Luft – Ballone und Luftschiffe* by Haaland, Knäusel, Schmitt and Seifert, Volume 26 of the series *Deutsche Luftfahrt* released by Dr. Theodor Benecke(†) in cooperation with the Deutsches Museum, the Federal Association of the German Aerospace and Space Travel Industry, Bonn, and the German Society for Air and Space Travel – Lilienthal-Oberth, Bonn, and published by Bernard & Graefe, Bonn 1997 (ISBN 3-7637-6116-4).

The Zeppelin story is told in a broad arc, with constant reference to the extensive literature, enabling the interested reader to complete his own picture. After a biographical sketch of Graf Zeppelin and a brief description of the creation of the Zeppelin group of companies, the design and technical development of the Zeppelin airships are described. Three dates define their history: Graf Zeppelin's initial idea in 1874, verified by written records, is at the beginning; there is a marker in the year 1900 when the first Zeppelin airship flew; and 1937, the year of the *Hindenburg* disaster, marks the end of Zeppelin airship travel. Brief chapters are dedicated to the construction of airships in other countries – at least those that used the Zeppelin method – and to the landing masts and hangars that were indispensible for the large airships. The appendices include notes from the various chapters, a list of sources, a register of names and a tabular overview of all the Zeppelin airships with vital data.

The Publisher

Introduction

Ferdinand Count von Zeppelin, builder of airships, is one of the German personalities from the turn of the 19th and 20th Centuries whose memory has stayed alive to the present day. With the exception of Kaiser Wilhelm II,[1] during whose reign the formative period of the Zeppelin airship took place, no other contemporary has received as much media attention as the Swabian count and his fascinating designs. Professor Henry Cord Meyer observed that, for Germany, he had been "its greatest popular hero since Bismarck."[2] The Zeppelin literature encompasses technical descriptions, monographs, biographies and political treatments, as well as descriptions of trips, novels, picture books, children's books, countless articles in newspapers and magazines, "secret" and widely-distributed printed materials with lectures, speeches, scientific experiments and the like. Pamphlets are quite rare. Even today new books and essays appear regularly, while old ones are reprinted. The number of publications in other languages, especially English is also considerable. Does it make any sense, therefore, to tell the Zeppelin story again? Well, the continuing requests alone appear to justify the project. But apart from that, the Zeppelin airships are undoubtedly an important part of German aviation history, indeed of contemporary German history itself, which – after an interval of decades – can and must be examined more critically than before. Delving into the wealth of Zeppelin literature, however, one encounters many inconsistencies.

Graf Zeppelin with his daughter Hella in the gondola of LZ 3 on 26 September 1907.

The only direct competition from inside Germany came from the Schütte-Lanz airships, however neither they nor their maker came close to achieving the popularity of the count and his "Zeppelins," as the giants in the sky became known in common parlance soon after their appearance. Today even the Schütte-Lanz airships are simply called "Zeppelins," as are the non-rigid blimps used for advertising, even though their shape is their only resemblance to Graf Zeppelin's airships and they share neither their size nor their technology. Peter Kleinheins made an amusing comment about this mix-up, which airship enthusiasts take pleasure in mocking: "Would anyone would make the mistake of calling a diesel a gasoline engine? But if a small non-rigid airship floats past, everyone says: 'Look, a Zeppelin!' The Zeppelin enthusiast should not take this as an insult, but rather as a complement: Zeppelin is now synonymous with the airship because of the achievements of the big airships,

Graf Zeppelin (left) is received by Kaiser Wilhelm II after landing in Berlin in LZ 6 on 29 August 1909.

which have fascinated our contemporaries for three decades."[3] The always and everywhere euphoric enthusiasm unleashed by the gigantic airships was due less to their performance than to the fascination they exuded, something clearly revealed by the Zeppelin literature.

It is interesting that, with its vast scope, the specialized Zeppelin literature has no particularly sophisticated element. The trivial dominates by a wide margin. The triviality is characterized by a more or less acceptable Zeppelin picture, distilled by constant rewriting and reformulation, which is beautiful and shining; transparency has suffered as a result, however, for the count and his airships are depicted as the authors would like them to have been, not how and what they were.

King August von Sachsen (center with walking stick) visits Graf Zeppelin in Friedrichshafen on 9 September 1909; left Ferdinand von Zeppelin Jr., a nephew of the count.

With the exception of purely technical treatments such as those by Ludwig Dürr,[4] Dietrich Engberding[5] and Wilhelm Ernst Dörr,[6,7] which are reliable sources, isolating the so-called specialist literature is difficult. All too often, even serious authors succumb to the fascination of the "silver fishes in the sky" and project their flawless appearance onto their creator and his colleagues. In this respect caution is called for. The Zeppelin biographies by August von Parseval,[8] Alfred Colsman[9] and Hugo Eckener[10] are among the best, as their authors knew the count personally and do not gloss over events. Hans von Schiller,[11,12] who can be added to this group, is unsurpassed with regard to statistics, which almost forms its own category of Zeppelin Literature. Other authors pursued completely different intentions as they viewed the subject with scientific detachment, for example Bernd Jürgen Warneken's[13] "case study," the critical depiction of the Zeppelin myth in Friedrichshafen by Martin Schmolze,[14] or the little known works by Elmar L. Kuhn[15,16] and Oswald Burger[17] on the societal, political and economic effects of airship construction. Such and similar fairly recent works show that the topic is still up in the air and far from being exhausted.

In the forefront are the few authors who, in recent times, have critically examined the Zeppelin airship program in its entirety in the context of its time and thus portrayed it in the proper light, Karl Clausberg and Henry Cord Meyer to name but two. Clausberg describes the Zeppelin airship company from its beginnings until the dinosaur-like extinction of the airship at the height of its technical perfection,[18] while, without losing sight of the facts, depicting the mass psychological reactions unleashed by the Zeppelins. Meyer gives a complete and unvarnished description of the events surrounding the Zeppelin airship company and interwoven political relationships,[19] He clearly depicts the military intentions Graf Zeppelin, who supported the notion that the harshest war was the mildest whilst referring to his airships as "ultimate weapons,"[20] and puts in their place all those authors who uncritically glorify the count, his colleagues and his work – which is the majority of them. After the analyses by

Graf Zeppelin with Korvettenkapitän Peter Strasser, the "Commander of Airships", in the gondola of navy airship L 4 (LZ 27) at the beginning of the First World War.

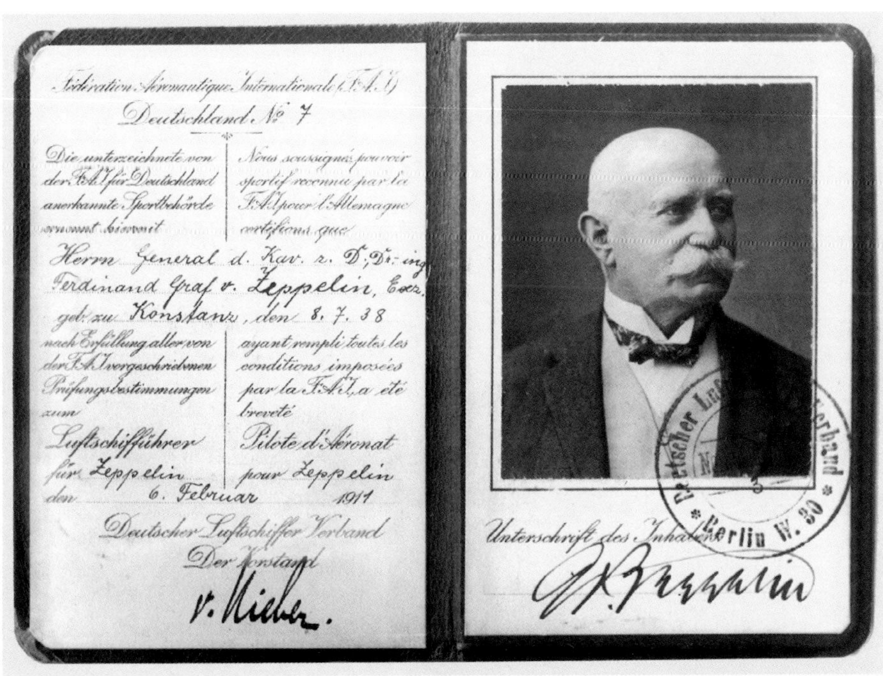

Fédération Aéronautique Internationale (F.A.I.)
Deutschland № 7

Die unterzeichnete von der F.A.I. für Deutschland anerkannte Sportbehörde [illegible]	Nous soussignés pouvoir sportif reconnu par la F.A.I. pour l'Allemagne certifions que

Herrn General d. Kav. z. D.; Dr.-ing. Ferdinand Graf v. Zeppelin, Exz. geb. zu Konstanz, den 8. 7. 38

nach Erfüllung aller von der F.A.I. vorgeschriebenen Prüfungsbestimmungen zum	ayant rempli toutes les conditions imposées par la F.A.I., a été breveté
Luftschiffführer für Zeppelin	Pilote d'Aéronat pour Zeppelin

den 6. Februar 1911

Deutscher Luftschiffer Verband
Der Vorstand
v. [illegible]

Unterschrift des Inhabers
[illegible]

International airship master's license, made for Graf Zeppelin on 6 February 1911.

Clausberg and Meyer, there is little room left for authors wanting to depict the Zeppelin history as a whole, without appearing superfluous. In the past it has seldom been pointed out that, while the Zeppelin airship company produced tremendous, in some cases brilliant technical solutions and provided many stimuli, the concept had so many inherent weaknesses that – with or without non-flammable helium – it was doomed to fail, not least because of economic reasons, and was ultimately a "dead end."[21] It is for this reason that the decades since the loss of the airship LZ 129 *Hindenburg* have not seen the realization of new operational large airships, even though the subject has been discussed around the world, inventors have worked on numerous projects and the modern technical possibilities are incomparably better than before. The building of large airships is a thing of the past.

Making a satisfactory choice of reading material is not easy. With one eye on the usable material and another on the dearth of secondary literature, Clausberg makes this clear in his introduction to his sparse list of literature and sources: "Even with the best of intentions, working with the patient gait of a scientific mill animal through a theme that is in the air like the Zeppelin history, would have become a Sisyphean labor."[22] He is therefore setting limits – but they cannot be free of subjectivity. In addition, it has to be noted that, in the author's view, the few secondary literature publications mentioned in the text – undoubtedly an important component of the total Zeppelin picture – should be identified by context without the intention of discriminating. Hopefully, by means of the printed materials and my own interpretation, I have succeeded in creating a relatively well-rounded picture of the history of the Zeppelins despite all of these reservations, difficulties and subjective assessments.

A Cavalry General Becomes a Builder of Airships

The life of Graf (Count) Zeppelin initially followed paths predetermined by ancestry and upbringing. The second half of his life was unusual, but that is understandable considering the period at the turn of the 19th and 20th Centuries. With technological advancement, the idea of flying took on increasingly concrete forms. After initial rejection, the unconventional path taken by Graf Zeppelin to realize the ancient dream of humanity found fertile ground in an imperialistic Germany that felt itself called to higher things.

Ferdinand Adolf Heinrich August von Zeppelin came into the world on 8 July 1838 in Konstanz on the shore of Lake Constance, the second of three children born to Count Friedrich von Zeppelin (1807-1886) and his wife Countess Amélie (1816-1852), nee Macaire d'Hoggeur. The children spent a comfortable childhood at Castle Girsberg not far from Konstanz in the Swiss canton of Thurgau. The father, an enthusiastic farmer, had marked musical interests. He and priest Robert Moser, considered a progressive, who raised Ferdinand after 1850, probably laid the groundwork for the diversity of interests that characterized his life. The mother was described as kind, intelligent and temperamental. A reading of the many Zeppelin biographies, such as those by Vömel, Hildebrandt, Rosenkranz, Eckener, Italiaander[1] and others, reveals that the family ties must have been very deep. This is underlined by a compendium of confidential Zeppelin family correspondence[2] found in Girsberg Castle in 1984, extracts from which were turned into a book. In 1869 he married Baroness Isabella von Wolff. Daughter Hellene (Hella), the later Countess von Brandenstein-Zeppelin, was born in 1879.

Ferdinand Graf von Zeppelin became a career soldier. As a young soldier, in 1863, at his own request, he went to the Unites States for a few months. He hoped to gain experience in modern warfare as an observer attached to the army of the northern states during the American Civil War. The sometimes adventuresome accounts of this trip are based entirely on his own descriptions,[3] which do not always stand up under reexamination, but which could also have been due to transcription errors.[4] In 1866, as a Württembergian officer, he fought on the side of Austria and its allies in the war against Prussia, and as a Württembergian *Hauptmann* we find him on the side of the Prussians in the war against France in 1870-71. One of his first military actions was a much-discussed cavalry patrol under his leadership. The action brought him effusive literary praise;[5] just a few years ago an admiring author revisited this theme,[6] although Zeppelin's headstrong behavior earned him criticism from his superiors. In any case, unlike the other members of the patrol, he was not decorated.

After the war he held a number of military positions. Zeppelin obviously also possessed marked negotiating skills, consequently both military and political careers lay open to him. From 1885 to 1887 he was the military representative of the Württembergian legation in Berlin. In 1888 King Wilhelm II of Württemberg made him *General à la suite*, and in 1889 he was Württembergian minister and representative in the *Bundesrat* (Federal Council). While he had always been interested in political affairs, the political tasks given him never held great importance in his life, even if he carried them out with a matter-of-fact dutifulness. Replacing military tunic with tails and top hat was difficult for him. After leaving the diplomatic service at the beginning of 1890, he busied himself with a subject that was received with much indignation in military circles. Rudolf Herzfeld wrote: "In this unemployed period, he picked up a hot potato which was repeatedly the subject of opposition and lively discussion in the Württembergian ministry of war, and which Graf Zeppelin also raised several times with the Prussian State Secretary Herbert von Bismarck: the absolute power of the Prussian commanding general. In 1890 he summarized his thoughts in a memorandum, the main theme of which was opposition to the idea of a commanding general named by the Prussians completely deciding the fate of Württembergian officers, and of the king being forced into the role of certifier. This situation must have disastrous results for the kingdom and, as a consequence, for the empire as well. In 1890, with the approval of the Württembergian war ministry, the memo was submitted to the Prussian foreign ministry as a personal expression on the part of the count. The results of the memo were resoundingly negative. It made it to the highest levels and evoked considerable indignation among the Prussian generals. The Kaiser himself expressed dismay over the "particularistic ideas" expressed in the memorandum. Faster than one might think, Graf Zeppelin was no longer 'acceptable.'"[7]

And so his career as a soldier came to a, for him, unsatisfactory conclusion. Herzfeld: "Even before the count received his promised transfer to the 30th Cavalry Brigade in Saarburg, there was talk in the inner circles that he was now not going to be made brigade commander. For Graf Zeppelin, the final act of this drama came during the autumn maneuvers of 1890, in which he had to demonstrate the command of an assembled cavalry division. In the maneuver critique his performance as a troop commander was given scathing criticism, and he was subsequently relieved of command."[8] On 29 December 1890, not long after he was promoted to *Generalleutnant*, Zeppelin left the army. He was permitted to retain the rank of *General à la suite* of the King of Württemberg, proof of the affection his sovereign felt for him.

This initially bitter fact did, however, give him the opportunity to dedicate himself to his airship idea, which had interested him for many years. His inspiration was Heinrich von Stephan,[9] who in 1874 had given a speech to the Scientific Society in Berlin with the very foresighted title of "Airship Travel and Universal Mail." In it, he prophesied the advent of steerable airships, which in his opinion would serve as fast mail carriers. His bold ideas were greeted on the one hand with skepticism, while on the other they provoked excitement, as in the case of Johann Schütte,[10] later to become Zeppelin's rival: "His [Stephan's] speech was likely one of the most interesting, most profound and most remarkable of the time about aviation, and the outstanding way in which the Secretary of the Imperial Post Office predicted or anticipated events in this field it is astonishing."[11] In May 1914, Graf Zeppelin once again declared to the Society of Naval Architects and Marine Engineers in Stuttgart: "The great importance that safe, long-range airships must achieve, was first revealed to me in the speech by Secretary of the Imperial Post Office Stephan, which was published as 'Universal Mail Airship Travel' in 1874. He

Ferdinand Graf von Zeppelin in 1887 as a Württembergian deputy in Berlin.

awakened in me the desire to make such ships a reality."[12]

In fact, the first verifiable mention of an airship, accompanied by a still very crude drawing, appears in Zeppelin's almost lifelong written journal of daily events and thoughts on 25 March 1874. From then on, the idea never left him. Although design solutions were still far in the future, in April 1875 he optimistically wrote: "While the procurement costs will be high, the operating costs will be insignificant. In the beginning, airship travel will in part be luxury enjoyment, in part merely the advent of what land and sea transport are unable to offer, namely a safe, easy and fast link between two points. The generalization of this new means of travel will undoubtedly not be long in coming."[13]

This would be realized for another twenty-five years, and, as we know, the "generalization" of airship travel as envisioned by the count never happened. Nevertheless, the fact that Zeppelin pushed his ideas through in the face of resistance from many quarters is admirable. In the end, the development of aviation as a whole profited from it, and many other branches of technology benefited from Zeppelin's developments in airship construction.

The years after the count's discharge from the military were filled with tremendous difficulties. Almost no one took him seriously. He had to rely on the financial assistance from others to build his first airship, but the applicant was rejected almost everywhere. The idea of a ship in the air, which was to be a hundred meters or even twice as long, seemed too bizarre. He was ridiculed as the, "fool of Lake Constance." It was not until he was successful and the first "Zeppelin" appeared in the sky, that the page gradually turned. The ultimate change in opinion took place in August 1908. The fourth Zeppelin airship had completed a much-watched flight of twelve hours duration over the Lake Constance area and Switzerland, and now it was to undertake a twenty-four-hour endurance flight. This was a condition for the military to place an order with the Zeppelin works. But the operation was a failure. After an involuntary landing because of engine trouble, the airship reached Mainz as planned and was on the return flight when an engine again failed. The crew landed in Echterdingen for repairs. There, with success within reach, the airship went up in flames during a thunderstorm. The flight had received a great deal of publicity beforehand, hundreds of thousands had watched and celebrated it, and now it appeared that the oft-prophesied end of the Zeppelin-Luftschiffbau had come. The recent flights had, however, obviously ignited the admiration and enthusiasm of elements of the population, and, as a result, events took an unexpected turn. Within a few weeks, six-million *Reichsmark* in donations flowed into Friedrichshafen, forming the basis of "an improbable success story,"[14] one with few equals. Immediately after the accident in Echterdingen, Kaiser Wilhelm II, who had previously shown only a rather lukewarm interest in Zeppelin's ideas, spontaneously and contemptuously described him as "the stupidest of all south-Germans." Graf Zeppelin must not have heard about this unkind remark, which was recorded by Prussian Court Marshall Robert Count von Zedlitz-Trützschler,[15] because the latter's writings were not published until 1923. The Kaiser soon pulled back, however. In the face of public opinion, three months later during a visit to the factory on Lake Constance he presented Zeppelin the Order of the Black Eagle.[16] The Kaiser zealously characterized him as "one of the greatest Germans of the century," while children recited the rhyme:

Zeppelin here, Zeppelin there,
Zeppelin has no airship anymore.
Zeppelin high, Zeppelin low,
Zeppelin has his airship again.
Zip-zap-Zeppelin,
the airship is back again.

Such lyrics appeared in great numbers in those days and were by no means limited to children's rhymes. On the contrary, multi-verse poems whose contents glorified Graf Zeppelin, his airships and the Fatherland made the rounds everywhere.[17] The popularity that Ferdinand Graf Zeppelin now enjoyed was unrivalled. He had become a cult figure in Germany around which everything seemed to turn, for "when, after a lengthy development phase and many failures, the Zeppelins were finally operable, in the national exuberance of the Wilhelmine era they were regarded as a typically German accomplishment; for a few decades they were, so to speak, a trademark for Germany."[18]

Zeppelin's popularity thus had a fertile breeding ground, which simultaneously nourished several ideas. With the design of rigid airships, Germany appeared to have risen to the apex of the industrial nations; no other country could boast a comparable technical feat, which also fulfilled the ancient human dream of flight. Another notion, one powerfully fomented by the count, was that Zeppelin airships would be an immensely effective weapon of war. For a long time England had dominated the world's oceans with her fleet. Kaiser Wilhelm had begun a massive shipbuilding program, but suddenly the airships seemed to open unforeseen possibilities in a war against England. The island kingdom was no longer safe from attack. It was believed that not only would the airships hold the English fleet in check from the air, but they would also be able to bring the nation to its knees with bombs. Graf Zeppelin himself first suggested the idea in his writings in 1866 and from then on spoke of it often and usually very forcefully. Hugo Eckener pointed out that in the spring of 1887 Zeppelin sent a memo to the king of Wurttemberg he had written after the successful flights by the Frenchmen Renard and Krebs in their non-rigid airship *La France*.[19] Zeppelin pointed out the, in his opinion, absolute necessity of building large, steerable airships, which were essential[20] for "the true exploitation of free airship flight for military purposes." Eckener continued: "From then on this idea, that the steerable balloon would become a very important instrument in the future prosecution of war, and that therefore Germany should spare no effort to become superior to its neighbor in this respect, began to dominate the count more and more and is what drove him to devote his free resources to the designing of an airship that would meet all the military requirements. The following sentence resonated in all the statements, ripostes, publicity, and insistent entreaties which he was to direct at a seemingly endless series of prominent and influential German men in the years that followed: "Help me build the airship for Germany's defense and security!"[21] The boon of donations after Echterdingen made it possible: a new class of weapon became operational. The fact that, after apparent initial success, it failed and only claimed senseless victims among the civilian population and the lives of many airship crews, did nothing to diminish Zeppelin's popularity until long after his death. He died in Berlin on 8 March 1917 of pneumonia following an operation.

History of the Zeppelin Company

The Zeppelin airship could only be realized and developed if a solid company undertook this task. The financial means required were enormously high, the prospects of success, however, very uncertain. The creation of an airship-building company was therefore probably one of the most difficult tasks that Graf Zeppelin had to cope with in his life. As additional companies for special tasks were soon created, qualified management personnel also had to be found or trained.

Alfred Colsman.

From the Beginnings to the Zeppelin Foundation

In December 1895 the count tried to raise at least 800,000 Marks, necessary for the construction of his first airship, by issuing credit notes in denominations of 20 Marks and more. Originally it was to have been a million, but from the beginning they cut back their expectations. Hugo Eckener described this futile effort:

"Understandably the success was very modest. About 100,000 Marks was collected, mainly through subscriptions from a few old friends, including members of the Württembergian royal family. Perhaps one of the main reasons for the failure was that the war ministry was vigorously dissuading those in military circles from subscribing. It was the time when the count was being ridiculed as a fool and when those in Stuttgart derisively pointed fingers at him."[1]

Not until the Association of German Engineers (VDI) became interested in the project was Graf Zeppelin given some sort of hope. After a speech to the VDI in Stuttgart in February 1896, with King Wilhelm II of Württemberg[2] in attendance, the association delved more deeply into his objectives. On 30 December 1896, "after deeper analysis of all the facts," it published an "appeal" for German industry, in particular, to support Zeppelin's plans.[3] It stated: "... The goal of these efforts [to build airships] is: safe transportation in the atmosphere, independent of roads of any kind, at speeds previously unattained. As distant as this goal may still appear today, everyone who thinks that it is physically and technically feasible will consider the many sacrifices and efforts worthwhile. One will only be able to approach this goal step by step, as in all previous cultural advances. In the opinion of leading experts, which we share, one such step would be the construction of an air vehicle based on Zeppelin's design and the preceding experimental research. It appears ruled out that the considerable sums of money necessary to initiate such steps can be laid out by individuals or minority shareholders. ... Therefore hope can only be placed in the charitable and selfless predisposition of those circles, and in particular of representatives of German industry, that might be prepared to raise the means for the funding of a very important and great technical mission of our age, without which a decisive step forward cannot be expected."

Despite this strong recommendation, donations were slow in coming, but a start had been made. The Society for the Promotion of Airship Travel was established in Stuttgart in June 1898. The list of stakeholders, however, contained just sixty-five names. In order to amass the necessary start-up capital, Graf Zeppelin was forced to purchase 441 shares each with a value of 1,000 Marks.

The society made possible the erection of a hangar, construction and three flights by the airship, but it had to be liquidated in early 1901 because the funds had been used up. On 30 March 1901 the liquidator of the company, Ernst Uhland, wrote a letter to Zeppelin which illustrates how difficult, indeed dramatic, the situation was: "Your Excellency, we have the honor to submit to you the enclosed bill for the minor and balance expenses incurred by you in the month of March in the sum of 29.70 Marks, as well as Herr Dürr's receipt for his March salary of 185 Marks. Further, we submit the enclosed account statement as of today, according to which you owe us a balance of 0.08 Marks. We ask that you review this and verify its correctness and submit an advance payment in cash in the near future to cover the expenses for April 1901 (approx. 1,000 Marks)."[4] The count immediately paid the eight Pfennigs to the company with, "... an additional 16.70 Marks, which are gratefully being using to settle the remaining debit balance with the Greisheim-Elektron chemical factory in Frankfurt a.M.," as Uhland immediately confirmed.[5] Despite this precarious situation, Graf Zeppelin continued to act enterprisingly. He once again invested his own capital, acquired funds from various sources and in 1905 began building additional airships. As previously mentioned, the fourth of these was involved in a spectacular accident in 1908 and surprisingly brought him six-million Marks.

Wilhelm Maybach

Karl Maybach

His finances bolstered, on 8 September 1908 Graf Zeppelin founded the Luftschiffbau Zeppelin GmbH (LZ) (Zeppelin Airship Construction Limited Liability Company).[6] He named Alfred Colsman,[7] the son-in-law of the aluminum maker Carl Berg,[8] managing director. And on 30 December 1908, Zeppelin took an important step to secure donor funds. He signed a document creating the Zeppelin Foundation, which still exits today under the administration of the city of Friedrichshafen.[9] The foundation's purpose was to support the construction of a new airship and "efforts to promote airship travel and its utilization for science." The last paragraph directed that the city of Friedrichshafen administer the foundation in the event that the purpose of the foundation could no longer be fulfilled.

Financially, nothing now stood in the way of building airships. It soon turned out that a growing number of very different problems had to be solved. To deal with these, "... Zeppelin developed a business concept that still appears modern today. Instead of concentrating all activities at the *Luftschiffbau* in Friedrichshafen, he established specialized subsidiary companies in each area of responsibility. 'Reducing production depth', as it is called today, was thus not an invention of Japanese industry."[10]

Of the many companies that were established, the most important are described below in the chronological order in which they were founded.

Graf Zeppelin around 1913.

A Group of Companies Is Created

In-House Production of Engines

In the early years, engines were still very unreliable and often placed the airships in danger. A solution had to be found quickly. This did not appear especially problematic, because a number of specialists were already actively involved in this field. They of course saw a great opportunity to advance their work through the building of airships. Karl Maybach,[11] the son of Wilhelm Maybach,[12] the former technical director and chief designer of the Daimler-Motorengesellschaft, designed an airship engine and asked the airship builders in Friedrichshafen to join an experimental company for the building of the engine. The Luftfahrzeug-Motorenbau GmbH was established in Bissingen near Stuttgart in March 1909, becoming the first subsidiary of the Luftschiffbau Zeppelin GmbH. In 1912 production was shifted to Friedrichshafen, and the company, which by then was not just building engines for airships, was renamed Motorenbau GmbH. Karl Maybach became co-partner and technical managing director. In 1918 the company received the name Maybach Motorenbau GmbH. During the First World War it also built large numbers of aircraft engines that were renowned for their reliability. Of the total of 119 Zeppelin airships built, the Types LZ 1 to LZ 8 plus the LZ 129 and LZ 130[13] were equipped with Daimler engines. All the rest were equipped with Maybach engines.

First Airline Company in the World

Among the early companies established by Luftschiffbau Zeppelin was the Deutsche Luftschiffahrts AG (DELAG), which was founded in Frankfurt am Main on 16 November 1909. As the first airline company in the world, it holds a special place in aviation history. Alfred Colsman drew up the establishment plan, after LZ 3, with twenty-five persons on board, completed a much-marveled-at eight-hour flight in March of the same year. This success voiced euphoric, and today it is difficult to imagine how much confidence there must have been in the business to make the decision to establish the company at that time. After all, LZ 4's accident in Echterdingen was only a few months in the past.[14]

It was hoped that DELAG, of which Alfred Colsman became the first managing director, would be the start of a continuous and lucrative business in the sale of commercial airships in large numbers, especially as Zeppelin was still waiting in vain for serious military contracts, the army having taken delivery of just a single airship. A condition for the business was, however, that enough cities build airship hangars to enable a regular air service plus sightseeing tours to be established. By the beginning of the First World War, airship hangars were built (in order of their completion) in Dusseldorf, Gotha, Baden-Oos, Berlin-Johannisthal, Frankfurt-Rebstock, Hamburg-Fuhlsbüttel, Leipzig and Dresden. This could have been the basis for a regular inter-city service, but realization of the plan was not as simple as imagined when DELAG was created. Not only were there not enough airships, which often crashed soon after they were completed, but there were also insufficient qualified flight crews and trained handling personnel. The required meteorological knowledge was also underestimated, and for the most part operations had to be limited to sightseeing trips. Nevertheless, by the outbreak of war almost 1,600 flights had been made and about 34,000 persons carried. From 1911 this included DELAG training personnel as well as members of the army and navy. Nevertheless, there were scarcely more than 10,000 paying passengers, which seriously dampened enthusiasm for the business. The accident rate was also high. Of the seven airships used by DELAG prior to the outbreak of war, four were lost in accidents.

The three airships built for the company after the war were significantly more capable than the prewar ships. Not only were considerable technical advances made during the war, progress was also made in operating technology. Despite impressive numbers, however, commercial operations could never be maintained without state subsidies. The Deutsche Zeppelin-Reederei (DZR) was founded in 1935, in which Luftschiffbau Zeppelin GmbH and Deutsche Lufthansa – and thus the Reich – were participants. The airships LZ 127 and the as yet uncompleted LZ 129 were brought in as capital. The founding of the firm was determined by tactical considerations.

"It is difficult to say with certainty who was the driving force behind the founding of this new company, the State Aviation Ministry in Berlin or the Luftschiffbau Zeppelin GmbH group of companies, which in the process virtually abandoned its air travel division. Both parties probably anticipated benefits, the state to gain a better insight into how and where its subsidies were used and be able to exert more influence on the use of airships, the Luftschiffbau Zeppelin GmbH group to acquire a strong partner for its popular, but no less loss-making problem child and to secure the future of commercial airship travel."[15]

Gas Cell Production

An intractable problem in the beginning was the manufacture of light, gas-tight cells for the hydrogen gas used to carry the airships. As the designers had to be stingy with every kilogram of weight, the rubberized fabric cells that were used caused considerable headaches on account of their weight. They also tended to build up an electrostatic charge, which posed a constant danger because of flying sparks, for in combination with the oxygen in the air, the hydrogen gas formed a highly-explosive oxyhydrogen. The solution was goldbeater's skin,[16] which was fabricated from the outer membrane of calf's intestine. It was gas-tight and extremely light when dry. In 1909 Zeppelin signed a contract with the Trenkmann Company of Berlin, which had experience in working with the material, and established the Ballonhüllen GmbH, in which Luftschiffbau Zeppelin GmbH held an 80% share. The attempt to mass-produce goldbeater's skin was successful, but soon there was insufficient space for the production of large gas cells, and in 1912 the Ballonhüllen-Gesellschaft GmbH was established in Berlin-Tempelhof.

The main problem that now arose was the procurement of sufficient quantities of calf's intestine, for the skins had to be laminated and at least 700,000 pieces were needed for a single airship of the size then being built. Calf's intestines were even procured from the depths of Russia. The gas cells were now very light, much less gas-porous and no longer accumulated a static electrical charge, but they were very expensive. A change was therefore made to a combination of goldbeater's skin and light cotton fabric.

Zeppelin and the Building of Aircraft

A firm that was not part of the Zeppelin group of companies but which owed its creation to Graf Zeppelin was the Flugzeugbau Friedrichshafen GmbH.[18] Zeppelin essentially created a competitor, which ultimately – in the long run – retained the upper hand. The count recognized the importance of aircraft early on, however. Exactly twenty years had passed since Dipl.Ing. Theodor Kober had made his airship idea a design reality. In 1907 he asked him to design an aircraft, to which he believed the future would belong. It was a view that his colleagues could not and would not believe. How foresighted he was is shown by a speech he gave to the German Shipbuilding Society in 1914. Zeppelin said that he had to, "... ask the entire aviation world, if aircraft would not take over the role of my airships and thus rob them of their *raison d'être*."[19] In his writings the

Theodor Kober

seventy-six-year-old even considered giving up the building of airships altogether and building "giant aircraft" instead. Understandably, neither the Luftschiffbau nor the Zeppelin Foundation was prepared to spend money on aircraft development, and so Zeppelin took matters into his own hands. He made the former shipyard facilities in Manzell near Friedrichshafen available to Kober and gave him a personal loan with which to establish the company. Kober achieved considerable success in a short time.

There Are no Hotels or Apartments

After Zeppelin began experimenting with his airships in Friedrichshafen, a steadily growing number of visitors came to the city. To accommodate the technicians, bankers and politicians, a comfortable house was built by the Kurgarten-Hotel GmbH, which was established specifically for that reason. It opened in 1910.[20] Tourism was driving the cost of living in the city to a record high, which led the workers to threaten strikes and mass demonstrations for the first time in 1911.[21] Unaffected by this, on 8 July 1913, the count's seventy-fifth birthday, Zeppelin proudly celebrated the achievements of his various companies. But now he was also to do something exemplary in the social field, and the Zeppelin-Wohlfahrt GmbH (Vowe Welfare Board) was established in Friedrichshafen, its main task being the building of apartments for company workers. The group also wanted to generate revenue through various personal contributions, especially in the field of agriculture, a concept that the work force accepted. Elmar L. Kuhn, however, wrote: "The establishment of the Zeppelin Welfare Board ... not only had a social side, rather its primary purpose was to help save consumer-market-regulating labor costs in the situation of the strained labor market."[22] And Kuhn also pointed out, "... that the original promise, to sell the houses to the residents, was later not kept, in order not to disturb 'the uniformity of the development' (Colsman). The houses were not completed until the war, and it was not until then and after the war that the Zeppelin Welfare Board achieved its full effectiveness."[23]

Four-engined R VI "giant aircraft" in Staaken near Berlin in 1917.

Architect Paul Bonatz[24] was placed in charge of design work. The so-called Zeppelin Village was built at the edge of the city not far from Luftschiffbau Zeppelin. Construction materials included bricks from the Grenzhof Brickworks, which was owned by the Zeppelin group of companies. The village consisted largely of single homes and duplexes, several shops, an inn and a communications center. Of the present-day situation of the ensemble, which is under a preservation order, Manfred Sauter wrote: "Unfortunately, the Second World War also inflicted significant damage in the Zeppelin Village. Some houses were totally destroyed and many were damaged to the degree that they were no longer habitable. Except for one, the houses were rebuilt or repaired according to original plans. It was advantageous that the entire village was still owned by the Zeppelin Charity Board, which wanted to preserve the basic substance and thus the overall character of the village."[25]

In-House Construction of Airship Hangars

With the advent of DELAG came the need for a growing number of airship hangars, and so in 1913, following the proven pattern, the Zeppelin-Hallenbau GmbH, Berlin was established, the last major concern founded before the war. The engineers' crowning achievement was bridging great spans with a minimum of building materials. During the war they even built a rotating hangar, in which two airships could be accommodated. Today, the airship hangar erected by the Gutehoffnungshütte Company for DZE according to Zeppelin-Hallenbau GmbH plans, at Santa Cruz near Rio de Janeiro, stands as an architectural monument. 250 meters long and 50 meters wide, in 1936 it was used to accommodate the airships LZ 127 and LZ 129.[26]

Establishment of Companies during the First World War

Zeppelin Promotes Claude Dornier

At the beginning of 1914, Graf Zeppelin asked Dipl.-Ing. Claude Dornier[27] to develop an all-metal airship for trans-oceanic use. Dornier, who designed airship hangars in the experimental department of the Zeppelin group's airship hangar company, where he experimented with aluminum sections that produced ground-breaking results for airship and aircraft construction, had impressed the count with his great technical abilities. The count had set up the experimental department himself and was a great supporter of the research program, even though many of his rather more practically-oriented colleagues had little use for it. In his Dornier biography, Joachim Wachtel wrote about a special experimental program: "In particular, its purpose was to achieve usable measurements from moving airships, which did not impress the old 'Zeppeliners'; in fact the entire experimental department was a thorn in their side. Practitioners like the experienced Ludwig Dürr, Zeppelin's chief designer, who possessed an uncommonly developed technical intuition, did not care for science. Dornier: 'Once, when I made reference to him of the results of my static calculations, he flared up and said: we don't need stress analysts, make a hundred trips in the ship before you have anything to say about it.'"[28]

Claudius Dornier

So that he could concentrate on development of the steel airship, Dornier was given his own department with the title "Zeppelin Luftschiffbau GmbH, Dept. Do." As the work would undoubtedly have taken several years, it was halted when the war began. Dornier was instead given the task of designing a multi-engine seaplane. The RS I flying boat was created in a hangar in Seemoos near Friedrichshafen and began trials on Lake Constance on 15 October 1915. It was powered by three Maybach engines each producing 249 HP (176 kW) and had a, for those times, huge wingspan of 43.5 meters. But development of this project, which was to have been the precursor of even bigger waterborne aircraft, could also not be continued on account of the war. Smaller, more nimble aircraft, like those built by the Flugzeugbau Friedrichshafen GmbH under Theodor Kober, were preferred by the military over larger types, which were untested and temperamental. The Saurer

Rs III First World War giant aircraft from Dornier.

automobile factory in Lindau was purchased, and the Do Department became the Zeppelin-Werk Lindau GmbH with Claude Dornier as managing director. In addition to RS-series flying boats it also built smaller aircraft. In 1920 Dornier became managing director of the new Dornier-Metallbauten GmbH, which rapidly gathered momentum, and in 1926 the Dornier-Flugzeug AG was formed in Altenrhein, Switzerland, also under Claude Dornier's leadership. Alfred Colsman was selected as chairman of the board. The giant Do X flying boat was created in Altenrhein and began flight trials in 1929. In 1932 all parts of the business went over to Claude Dornier, who became the sole shareholder. The discovery of Dornier as a designer and businessman was due to Ferdinand Graf Zeppelin. The stimuli Dornier gave to aviation have not received the recognition they deserve.

Alfred Count von Soden-Fraunhofen.

Shortage of Gears and Transmissions

In the early years of the war the enemy demonstrated great success in aircraft construction, which led the Heeresverwaltung (Army Administration) back to the use of more reliable reduction gears. As gears with the precision required for aircraft and airship construction were not available in Germany, in typical Zeppelin fashion the count established his own specialized company. In August 1915 the Luftschiffbau Zeppelin GmbH and Max Maag Zahnräder of Zurich, which had experience in manufacturing gears, signed contracts that resulted in the establishment of one of the most important companies in the Zeppelin group, the Zahnradfabrik GmbH Friedrichshafen. Alfred Count von Soden-Frauenhofen[29] was hired as technical managing director. In 1921 the company was turned into a joint stock company. Luftschiffbau Zeppelin acquired 80% of the shares, Max Saag the remaining 20%. In 1931 the company became Zahnradfabrik Friedrichshafen AG, whose abbreviation ZF the company retains to this day. From very modest beginnings in a factory barracks, the so-called *Zackenbude*, the company has risen to become a world-class concern. In his biography of Soden, Wolfgang Meighörner-Schardt observed that "the innovative élan of the young company under Count Soden, which was able to submit ten patents in its first year of existence," was ahead of its time.[30] Karl Clausberg explained the company's success: "Thanks to superior production technology – made possible by the machines of Swiss engineer Max Maag – the factory was in a position to design and deliver transmissions that were completely superior to any that had come before. The company was established too late to profit from war contracts."[31] After the war this could have led to the almost complete shutdown of the still young operation, but Soden was able to prevent it. Rudolf Herzfeld noted in his comprehensive history of the company: "Count Soden fought against the threatened closure of the company with all the means at his disposal. He tirelessly stressed to the shareholders that after the startup problems had been overcome, the company would be able to operate profitably, if they just helped it for a short stretch. In fact, ZF did not operate at a loss in 1918 despite all the difficulties caused by the war. The debt was an unavoidable consequence of high capital expenditures and the considerable licensing costs, which could not be expected to be obtained more cheaply in the first three years."[32]

Factories in Berlin

Although work in Friedrichshafen had been proceeding under high pressure since the start of the war and airships were being completed at shorter intervals, the war ministry pressed LZ to build an additional factory in order to produce more airships for military use. The company therefore built facilities for the construction of airships in Berlin-Staaken, where before the war the conglomerate, always ready to take risks, had acquired a large space for a "world airport," and in autumn 1915 it created the Luftschiffbau Zeppelin Staaken GmbH.[33] In order to be as rational as possible, a light-metal foundry and a gas plant were added. Of the total of 102 Zeppelin airships built for the army and navy, just twelve were made in Staaken, for before the operation was really up and running, it had been realized that the high losses being suffered by the airships did not justify the cost. The army stopped using airships in 1917 and the navy in the last year of the war. The facilities in Staaken were then used for the production of aircraft. The foundry and gasworks later became independent companies.

Large Aircraft or Zeppelins?

When the war began, Zeppelin repeated his call for large aircraft. On 6 August 1914 he wrote: "Lessons learned in the construction of aircraft, continuing improvements in engines and a newfound use of building materials make it possible to tackle aircraft with a range of 900 kilometers. Even if these aircraft are not at first able to observe, report wirelessly and shoot down enemy aircraft like the airships, they would be ahead of the airships by not using gas, which is not easily obtainable everywhere, or the very large hangars and could manage with much smaller crews. To prevent misunderstandings, however, I realize that it would be wrong to halt or even restrict the production of airships because of the prospect of powerful aircraft, for such aircraft have not yet been built or tested. But Dürr, Dornier and now also Klein and Bosch ... are convinced of the feasibility of powerful aircraft."[34]

Realization was not long coming. The Stuttgart manufacturer Robert Bosch made available to Zeppelin Gustav Klein, who was mentioned in the note, and several capable colleagues. They were brought together in the Versuchs GmbH in Gotha, which was established specifically for the purpose, with Klein as managing director. The first test flight by an R aircraft (R = *Riesen*, or giants) took place on 19 April 1915. Zeppelin was visibly pleased by this triumph: "Yesterday morning in Gotha, I was present for the first test flight by a large land aircraft (bomber). The project has been a success in every way. An excellent weapon has been created for Germany."[35]

In the summer of 1916 the operation moved to Berlin-Staaken and was renamed the Flugzeugwerft GmbH Staaken. The land for the company was procured from the Bodengesellschaft Hansa GmbH, a company formed specifically to acquire properties in Berlin. All shares in the company were held by LZ. In addition to giant aircraft, small aircraft were also produced in Staaken. In the spring of 1918 the Flugzeugwerft GmbH Staaken and Luftschiffbau Zeppelin Staaken GmbH were combined to form Zeppelin GmbH Berlin-Staaken.[36]

The Sawmill

There remain two more company foundations from the war years to be mentioned, the Propellerbau GmbH Berlin-Potsdam (1916) and the Holzindustrie Friedrichshafen GmbH, Mecklenburg Factory (1918). The attempt to operate a company for the manufacture of propellers based on a purchased patent was a failure, because it – an exception in the history of the conglomerate – lacked suitable management personnel and also workers.[37] The separate company established, in keeping with the policies of the conglomerate, to meet the large need by all of its various companies for timber and sawn wood, was, however, a success. Originally it was planned to erect a sawmill on the factory grounds in Friedrichshafen, but then a parquet and box factory was acquired in nearby Mecklenburg which could be converted for the purpose in mind.[38]

The Weimar Republic and the Nazi Period

A third founding phase followed after 1918. It was preceded by a consolidation process, for the conglomerate's structure had become difficult to manage and many companies abruptly fell into a production hole at war's end. This primarily affected the workers. Until the Zeppelin Welfare Board in 1908, Zeppelin had never employed more than seventy people. When the war began, about 800 were counted in the Zeppelin businesses, about 500 in LZ, 200 in engine construction and sixty in aircraft construction. By the end of the war, this number had increased phenomenally to more than 11,000.[39] The majority of them were not from the city of Friedrichshafen, but from the surrounding areas. The Zeppelin Welfare Board had built an extra rail line, the "*Teuringer Talbahn*," for these workers. Alfred Colsman, who ran the companies with an iron hand after Zeppelin's death in 1917, displayed an ice-cold, almost cynical behavior: "When the first news of the collapse of the front arrived, the group of companies' foreign workers were paid their wages and train fare and left immediately. In this way I got rid of a considerable part of the foreign elements."[40]

New Companies Are Created from Old Ones

The group's founding activities that now followed took place under different circumstances instead of under the pressure of wartime. The restrictions of the Treaty of Versailles affected the elements of the group, which had been mainly involved in the construction of airships and aircraft, especially hard. It instinctively adopted survival strategies in its new founding activities, which were often no more than the renaming, reduction or shifting of functions. Hugo Eckener, who had joined LZ as an advisor in 1908, played an especially prominent role. The count had noticed Eckener early on, when, as a correspondent for the newspaper *Frankfurter Zeitung* in 1908, he spoke out critically about the experiments with the first Zeppelin airship over Lake Constance.[41] Zeppelin then approached him, in order to win over the native of Flensburg to the airship idea. His involvement proved to be a great stroke of luck for LZ before and during the war, when the experienced sailor trained crews for the hard-to-navigate airships with a nautical flair. During the reorganization of the group structure after the war ended in 1918, Eckener displayed outstanding strategic talent, which enabled him to become one of the leading figures in the group next to Alfred Colsman. He then dedicated his efforts to saving as many parts of the group as possible. A typical example was the airship works in Staaken, whose use was no longer permitted. An effort was therefore made to split off the facilities there for producing hydrogen. October 1920 saw the founding of the Zeppelin-Wasserstoff- und – Sauerstoff GmbH (ZEWAS), which also produced acetylene gas and became involved in the manufacture of synthetic gemstones. The company was very successful. In 1923 it was turned into a limited stock company and for a long time was a valuable subsidiary of the group. Like ZEWAS, it was decided to separate the light metal forge from the Staaken airship works and place it on its own feet. In May 1921 the Zeppelinwerke Gießerei GmbH, Staaken was added to the commercial register. Its main customers for cast products were the automobile and engine industries.[42]

In order to get operations by the DELAG going again, in August 1919 the airship LZ 120 *Bodensee* entered service. It had a gas capacity of 20,000 cubic meters. The maximum allowable was 30,000 cubic meters, which was modest compared to the wartime airships, which reached up to 68,500 cubic meters. By order of the Allies, however, the ship was forced to cease operations in December 1919 and was handed over to Italy. Its sister ship, LZ 121 *Nordstern*, went to France even before it could enter service. Eckener's efforts to save the DELAG had thus failed, and it also seemed as if there was no way to save the Luftschiffbau-Zeppelin GmbH, especially as France and Great Britain, because of their civilian populations' bitter experiences with the Zeppelins during the war, demanded the destruction of all aviation facilities in Germany.

A Zeppelin for America

Hugo Eckener, who in contrast to Colsman's diversification strategy staked everything on the airship, did not give up. As the USA showed interest in airship construction and was interested in exploiting the experience of the builders from Friedrichshafen, he was able to delay the demolition of the facilities on Lake Constance. After tough negotiations he succeeded in gaining approval for the construction of an airship, to be taken into account against reparations owed to the United States. Now there was no more talk of demolition. LZ 126 was built, and in October 1924 it was flown to the USA, thus marking a milestone in the barely forty-year history of the Zeppelin.

Hugo Eckener.

The successful crossing of the Atlantic resulted in the founding of companies in the USA. On 19 September 1929 in Akron, Ohio, an agreement was signed for the founding of the Goodyear Zeppelin Corporation, with two-thirds of its shares owned by Goodyear Tire & Rubber and one-third by Luftschiffbau-Zeppelin GmbH. The company projected several large airships based on the Zeppelin system, of which two were completed. Eckener's efforts to establish a German-American airline failed, however, in part because both airships crashed.[43]

Looking back, Elmar L. Kuhn described the Weimar period as follows: "If you consider the history of the Zeppelin group, the years of the Weimar Republic were a sometimes critical transition phase between two armaments booms, with a stagnation phase and finally a downsizing phase between two growth spurts. If one ignores the following years, after the very different developments for the individual companies, by the end of the 1920s almost all of them were in a crisis that threatened their existence, from which economic developments hardly promised a way out." And the conclusion for the Luftschiffbau-Zeppelin group: "Airship construction itself had not found a sufficiently stable second mainstay and, with its aerial monsters, was dependent on government subsidies, like Dornier on state contracts for his more promising aircraft. Maybach could only be saved by the dieselization of rail traffic by the state railway. Progress in motorization and road building, on which Maybach and especially LZ were dependent, could also only be pushed through by corresponding government measures. With far more than half of production volume, the group was on the government drip, the smaller components of demand reacted by way of the market indirectly on government action. The government's austerity drive must hit the industries in Friedrichshafen especially hard, even if they got off lightly in all the austerity measures."[44]

Propaganda for the Nazis

After the Nazis came to power, March 1935 saw the creation of the previously-mentioned Deutsche Zeppelin Reederei GmbH (DZR) based in Frankfurt am Main. It was supposed to resume the activities of the defunct DELAG. Already in 1931, a scheduled air service between Friedrichshafen and Rio de Janeiro had been started with the LZ 127 *Graf Zeppelin*, and the more modern LZ 129 *Hindenburg*, with which it was planned to start regular North Atlantic traffic, was under construction. The Nazis hoped that voyages by the big airships would be propaganda coups. But the far-reaching plans by this company and all of LZ's subsequent plans burst asunder on 6 May 1937, when LZ 129 exploded shortly before landing at Lakehurst, New Jersey. The ultimate end of Zeppelin airship travel came on 6 May 1940.

On the third anniversary of the catastrophe in Lakehurst, DZR's airship hangars in Frankfurt were demolished. LZ 127 and LZ 130, which after the Lakehurst accident was completed but never carried passengers, had previously been scrapped in March and April. The Zeppelin people had previously held discussions with the Nazis in an effort to save their airships from destruction, all of them with Hermann Göring, who was an opponent of airships.[45] It was all in vain. The two Zeppelins were destroyed, but this action by the Nazis was in no way the end of the group – yet another founding phase was to follow.

The Destruction of Friedrichshafen

In Friedrichshafen, history first took its fateful course. Increasingly, life in the city was dominated by the Second World War. Instead of Zeppelins the company built military equipment. Among others things, LZ made parts for Wernher von Braun's infamous "revenge weapons."[46] Columns of forced laborers and concentration camp inmates were used for this in various companies. Oswald Burger, who has researched the topic of "Zeppelin and the armaments industry on Lake Constance," wrote about several internment and concentration camps in and around Friedrichshafen.[47] Nevertheless, with respect to the then customary subservience to the Nazis, he came to a moderate judgment of those in charge in the Zeppelin group: "Whereas it can rightly be said of the period before the First World War that "reckless bravado" characterized the leaders of the group and especially Graf Zeppelin,[48] who displayed an extreme identification with Wilhelmine Germany – such that the count sometimes had to be forced to show restraint – nothing similar took place during the Second World War. A reading of official statements by the leaders of the group of companies during the Third Reich reveals a definite coolness towards and distance from the Nazi ideology. Verbal concessions (like the unavoidable reverence for the Führer) very rarely appear in the speeches and commemorative publications from the National-Socialist period and then are separated from the remaining content, suggesting a certain distance.[49] On the other hand they were pleased to tacitly profit from the industrial promotion and production programs of National-Socialism and its rigorous policies against the workers."[50]

The group's companies suffered heavily from the Allied bombing. The first raid took place on 21 June 1943 and many more followed. For this reason most production facilities were evacuated from the city. By the end of the war the city of Friedrichshafen had largely been destroyed.

Development after the Second World War

After the end of the war, many former employees of the Luftschiffbau hoped that they would resume the construction of large airships, but Hugo Eckener rejected this suggestion as ivory tower thinking: "You must finally accept that the day of the airship is gone forever. If you continue wishing to hang on to the airship, it would mean the same thing as doing away with traffic on the highways and returning to covered wagons."[51]

Cooking Pots and Motor Vehicle Repair

Friedrichshafen was in the French occupation zone. The Luftschiffbau-Zeppelin GmbH was placed under French control. By the beginning of 1946 the clean-up work and retrieval of the machines and material had reached the stage that a modest program for civilian requirements could begin. Cooking pots and other simple cooking equipment was made. At the same time, LZ began repairing and overhauling the vehicles of the occupying power. Like after the First World War in Staaken, two operating branches were split off and made independent, the Friedrichshafen oxygen works as successor to the LZ Gasworks Department and the Friedrichshafen Metallbearbeitung.

On 1 January 1947, LZ, like many other former armaments producers, was forbidden to undertake production. Only the work for the French Army was permitted to continue, but not by LZ but instead by two new companies under French control, between which the majority of LZ's personnel were divided. The carousel of company foundations thus began to turn again – albeit under different auspices.

Various mergers led in 1950 to the Fahrzeug-Instandsetzung GmbH Friedrichshafen (FIF), which continued carrying out repair and servicing work, but also manufactured tank-trucks, various mechanical devices and paving machines for the Vögele Company. Interesting contracts were handmade automobile bodies. A rich American ordered a complete luxury limousine.

A group of LZ technicians under the direction of senior engineer Karl Walter got together in 1946 to design projects and make preparations for production. With LZ no longer permitted to produce after 1947, Walter and his people went to the C.H. Straub Company in Ravensburg, a metalworking business, which set up the "Walter Group," a department for the design of light metal structures. The multifaceted production program reflected the pioneering spirit of those early years that had been born out of adversity. Among the products made were gondolas for cableways, aluminum paddleboats, luggage racks for rail cars and much more. Even complete houses made of aluminum parts were built. In 1950 the department was taken over by the Zeppelin Foundation and brought into the Metallwerke Friedrichshafen GmbH. From it developed a special branch for the production of large containers, which today plays a leading role in the group under the name Zeppelin Silo/ Apparate Technik GmbH.[52]

The Group of Companies Today

An important step in the further development of the operations took place in 1954, when it became the exclusive representative of the American-based Caterpillar Tractor Co., today Caterpillar Inc., for the then Federal Republic and West Berlin. In 1961, when the Metallwerke Friedrichshafen was able to take over the FIF and the Burkhart Company in Ravensburg, a galvanizing company with which it had long worked, it as renamed the Zeppelin Metallwerke GmbH. The development of this company, which saw itself as the successor to the former airship-building company – the Luftschiffbau Zeppelin GmbH still exists as a capital management company under the Zeppelin Foundation – brought with it the founding of other companies, quite in the style of Graf Zeppelin, Alfred Colsman and Hugo Eckener. From the Zeppelin-Metallwerke GmbH, in 1994 the Zeppelin GmbH was created as a holding company, under which a number of companies with subsidiaries and associated companies were established in Germany and abroad as independent entities. Under the Luftschiffbau Zeppelin GmbH as chief partner was created the Zeppelin Luftschifftechnik GmbH, which is engaged in development of a "new technology" airship, the so-called "Zeppelin NT" (see Page 129).

The Zeppelin Airships

Zeppelin airships were the most significant representatives within the group of rigid airships. Their structure was characterized by a rigid frame with several independent gas cells in the interior and an outer shell which gave the vehicle an aerodynamic shape and protected the interior, especially the gas cells, from mechanical and weather-related influences. The most striking feature of the Zeppelin airships was their size (up to 245 meters long and more than forty meters in diameter), which has not been achieved by any other air vehicle to this day.

The huge dimensions were required to accommodate the large quantities of gas. The Schütte-Lanz airships in Germany and even several rigid airships in England and the USA shared these features.

A Word about Designations

The Luftschiffbau Zeppelin built a total of 119 airships between 1899 and 1938, for which the now typical type designation LZ (= Luftschiff Zeppelin) followed by an Arabic number from 1 to 131 (factory number) will be used in this book. Airship projects that were not completed were also numbered, which explains the difference in figures.

Contemporary model of the steerable air vehicle, for which Graf Zeppelin was awarded patent No.98580 in August 1895 (see page 33). The model has a motorized tractor unit (left), on which are mounted several carriers for the transporting of loads. Serving as an expert on behalf of the general staff, Rudolf von Tschudi of the Prussian Airship Battalion determined that a vehicle of this kind would encounter insurmountable design, technical and aerodynamic problems and advised against its adoption.

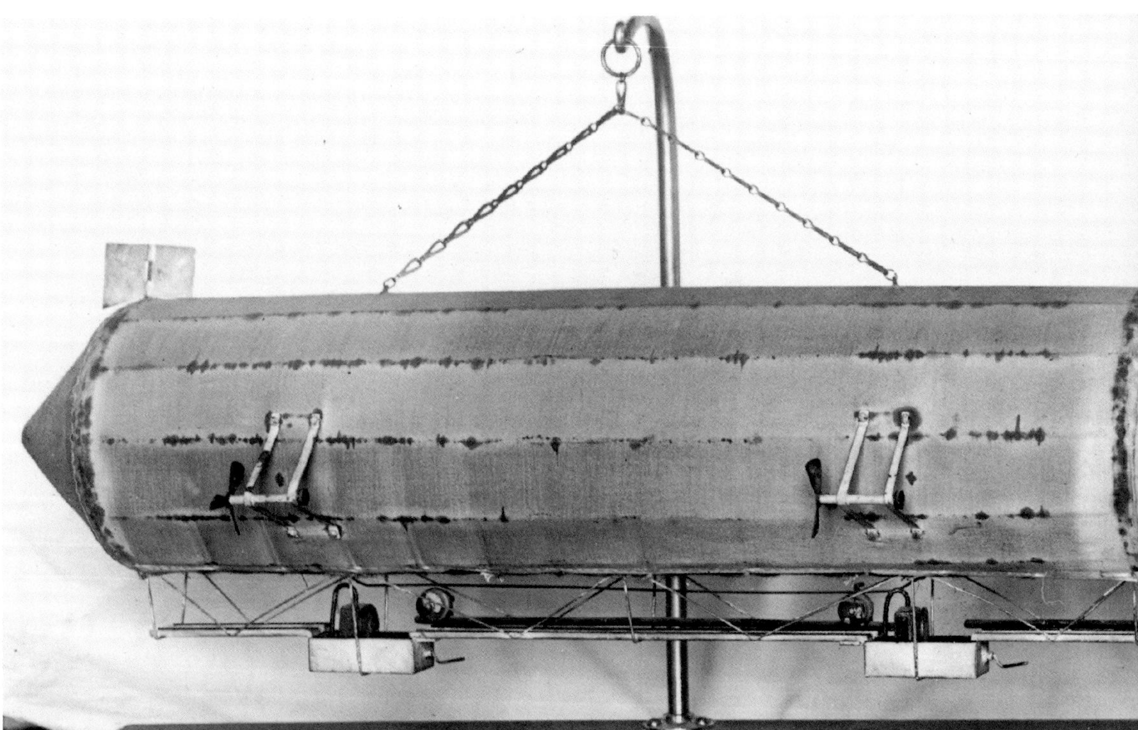

For reasons of secrecy, during the First World War military airships were given designations that deviated from this rule. In the beginning, those of the army were identified by a Z followed by a Roman numeral. This was later changed back to LZ with an Arabic but higher number than the consecutive factory number (plus 30). The navy's airships were designated with the letter L followed by a number that was lower than the factory number.

A total of twenty-seven different variants were built, which up until LZ 126 were identified within the company with an "a" to "z." The last Zeppelin airships had no such designation. The archaic-sounding LZ 1 did not differ from the last Zeppelins LZ 129 and LZ 130 in basic concept, but the technical advancements made in three-and-a-half decades of development were evident.

For this reason, the tangled and laborious history of the origins of the LZ 1 and its clumsy flight trials will be described in greater detail, and similarly a detailed description of the LZ 129 Hindenburg, the last Zeppelin airship used to carry passengers, will be given to illustrate the technology that existed at the end of the Zeppelin era. All of the other airships that were built will be described in less detail while stressing technical peculiarities, noteworthy performances and fates. Only LZ 126 and LZ 127 will be described in greater detail, in keeping with their place in the history of Zeppelin, not least because of the tremendous literary echo that these ships, like LZ 129, have found.

From Concept to First Ascent

According to several statements by its creator, the Zeppelin airship was no independent "invention," rather it was a conglomeration of diverse theoretical considerations and practical experiments by other airship builders. Like all those of his time interested in the subject of airships, Graf Zeppelin followed with interest the work of Henri Giffard, Paul Haenlein, Ernst Georg Baumgarten and Friedrich Hermann Wölfert, Charles Renard, Arthur Krebs[1] and many others.

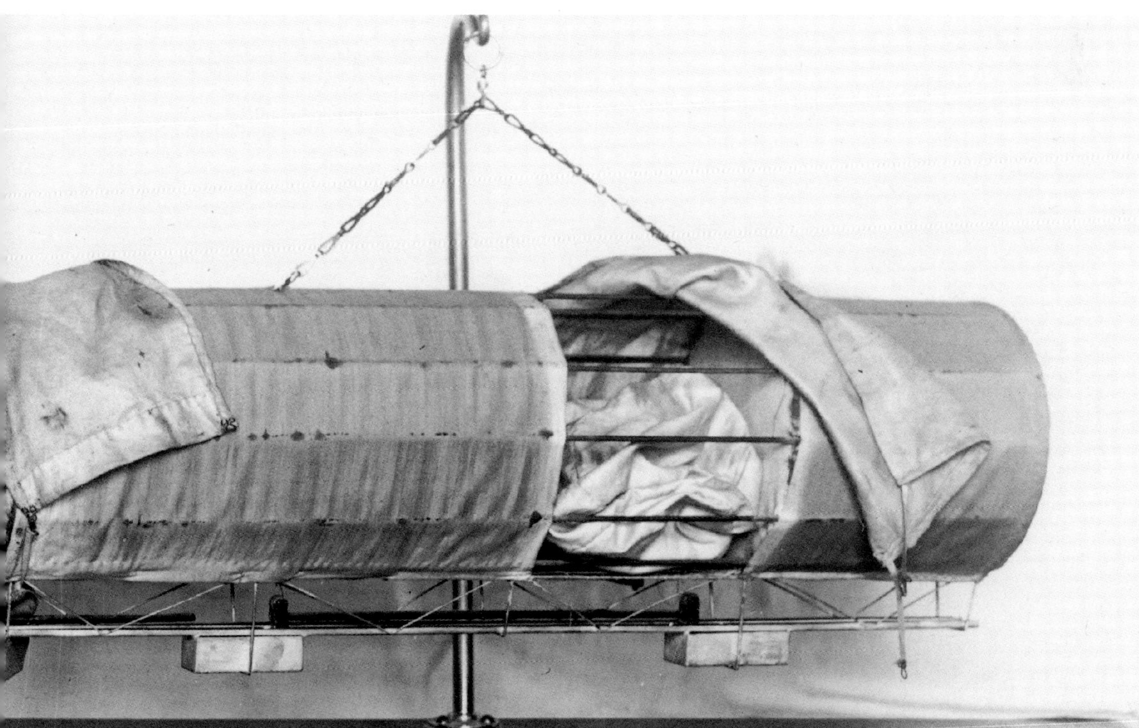

First Notes and Sketches

Zeppelin was a technical layman, but he soon realized that the potential performance of an airship was greatly dependant on its size. When he wrote his first memorandum dealing with the theme of airships – it is dated 25 March 1874, when Zeppelin was thirty-six years old – he already had this point in mind: "The vehicle would be designed with the dimensions of a large ship. The gas volume so calculated, that it would support the ship except for a slight surplus weight. Liftoff would be achieved by the power from the engines, which would, as it were, drive the vehicle on the upwards-positioned wings. On reaching the desired height, the wings would be positioned less steeply, causing the airship to remain in the horizontal plane. To descend, one would set the wings less steeply or allow speed to drop. Steering would probably best be achieved, with lowest possible design weight, through the use of canvas controls on the bow and stern."[2]

An analysis of these notes is interesting. The airship was to be as large as a big ship, whatever that was supposed to mean, but the gas volume so calculated that would be slightly heavier than air, not lighter. According to this text, lift would be created dynamically! Zeppelin was aware of the problem of weight and he addressed it in this memo, especially with reference to the control surfaces. He obviously possessed a well-developed sense of technical and physical processes. A drawing that accompanied the notes shows that, at that time, he had only rather vague idea as to what the gas body might look like, with the dimensions of a large ship and having to be extremely light, but the time was ripe for visions in this direction. With non-rigid airships, the maximum possible length of the lifting body, up to which its shape could remain stable, was very soon reached. Semi-rigid airships resulted in greater dimensions, but they too were only capable of carrying small payloads. The logical consequence, therefore, was an airship with a rigid lifting body, which would, however, have to have a length of 100 meters or more in order to lift itself and additional loads. Zeppelin certainly was certainly under no illusions, realizing that, given the current state of technology, achieving this requirement would be difficult, and so he came up with the idea of dividing the lifting body into smaller units and coupling them together, with the first unit designed as a tractor unit. The airship became an "air vehicle." Although none was ever built, Zeppelin himself clung to this designation for a long time.[3]

There was no shortage of ideas, but what good were all the definitions and sketches as long as no one showed any interest in the project? As one could easily imagine, financing would devour huge sums of money. It was obvious that, in these early stages, interested parties would have to be found in military circles, not in business. After lengthy efforts by the count, by 1891 the general staff was at least prepared to have a look at the project. The meeting with Rudolf von Tschudi[4] brought Zeppelin only disappointment, for Tschudi's investigations revealed that the planned vehicle's drag was much greater than expected, and with the weak power plants then available, construction would have been pointless. The count didn't let this discourage him, instead he did exactly the right thing, turning his attention to the engines, on which his plans obviously threatened to founder. He succeeded in winning over the Daimler-Motoren-Gesellschaft for the development of the lightest and most powerful power plants possible. This cooperation soon produced tangible results. In addition, Gottlieb Daimler[5] brought in engineer Theodor Groß, a specialist who was supposed to make the initial calculations for the airship. He was less than convinced by Zeppelin's ideas, however, and after a short time there was a parting of the ways.

Zeppelin was able to win over engineer Theodor Kober,[6] who had gained experience in the field of aviation with the Augsburg balloon maker August Riedinger.[7] From then on the ideas took on a more concrete form, at least on paper. Kober, a man with varied interests, went to work with reluctance. On one of his cost proposals dated 3 August 1893, he noted critically: "In order to avoid any sort of misunderstanding, I again point out that the design and manufacture of a practical vehicle is as yet in no way assured."[8]

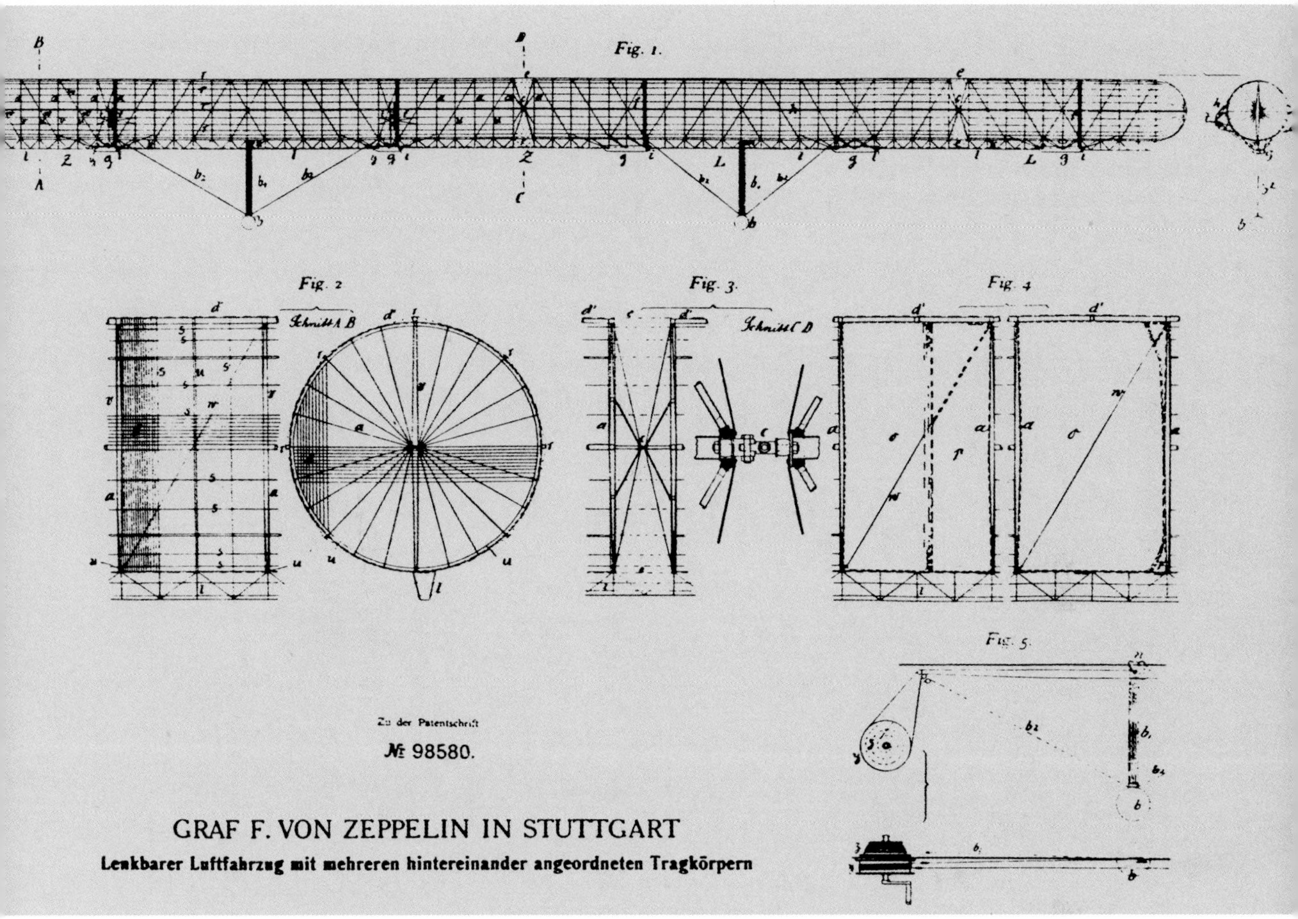

Drawing of the "steerable air vehicle with several carrier bodies arranged in tandem" from the patent specification No.98580 of 1895.

The Patent Specification

At that time the Austro-Hungarian timber merchant David Schwarz[9,10] was working on a rigid airship and used the then still little-known metal aluminum.[11] The Lüdenscheid manufacturer Carl Berg[12] experimented successfully with the industrial manufacture of this extremely light metal, and the Schwarz project suited him perfectly. Without his help it is unlikely that it would ever have come to fruition.[13] In connection with the Schwarz airship, there were later frequent accusations about the originator of the Zeppelin airship,[14] but it can be assumed that neither Zeppelin nor Kober considered an all-metal airship, while on the other hand Schwarz did not, for example, think of separate gas cells. As well, the Schwarz airship was first developed by engineer Carl Berg between 1892 and 1895, while Graf Zeppelin received his patent in 1895.[15] And this patent shows that Zeppelin and Kober were moving in a much different direction with their design than the Schwarz airship. First of all the patent specification meant something quite different to the count. Ludwig Dürr wrote: "For Graf Zeppelin, the issuing of the patent for his airship, which took place on 13 August 1898, three years after it was submitted, meant the vindication of his views in terms of public opinion. He then turned all his energy to making his project happen."[16]

The patent specification also bolstered Zeppelin's confidence on the way to his first airship, although it soon turned out that the patented invention would not be feasible. Zeppelin and Kober were forced to accept the conclusion reached by Tschudi that the idea of several lifting bodies coupled together and pulled through the air by a tractor unit would face insurmountable design, technical and aerodynamic difficulties. Nevertheless, the patent specification contained all the features that characterized the later Zeppelin airships, though not as patent claims. In this respect the patent specification aimed beyond the airships later built. Patent Specification 1, the main claim, stated:

"A steerable air vehicle, characterized by several flexibly-joined lifting bodies, of which the first accommodates the power plants and the others the payload, with the spaces between the lifting bodies covered with an elastic shell (e), which is attached to the rigid shells of the neighboring lifting bodies." The second patent specification concerned the arrangement of the power plants, in order to achieve a "relatively small cross-section of the [cylindrical] lifting body." Kober and Zeppelin obviously assumed that a slim cylinder would represent the most aerodynamic shape, which the patent examiner probably also saw. Johann Schütte,[17] who appeared as Graf Zeppelin's only competitor in Germany in the field of rigid airships, changed his design, building streamlined airships after 1908.[18] It is interesting that they wanted to use the technology of the non-rigid airship, for Patent Claim 3 read: "The air vehicle described in Claim 1, the introduction of special maneuvering gas envelopes (p), from which gas can be released as required, so that the gas envelope in the same chamber (o) takes the place of the maneuvering envelope, for the purpose of keeping constant the gas contents of the envelopes (o) and preventing them from becoming contaminated with air." In practice, however, Claim 4 made little sense. It concerned the arrangement of sliding weights suspended beneath the lifting bodies for trimming of the vehicle. The system was used in the first ascent by LZ 1, however in this form it had to be abandoned for the second test flight.

The patent specification is proof that the Zeppelin airship was not a Zeppelin invention – something the count himself never claimed – for its characteristic features were not elements of the patent specification. Instead they appeared in the explanatory text where, from the standpoint of patent law, they represented the "existing state of technology" and therefore nothing new, and thus were not or not again eligible for patent protection: "In order to give the airship a rigid shape, it is provided with a frame of tubes r, wire cables r and wire mesh d (Fig.1 and 2), over which is stretched an outer shell of silk or similar material. The interior of the frame is stiffened with bulkheads a, vertical struts v (Fig.2), and lying between these circumference rings and diagonal struts w. The mentioned bulkheads will divide the air vehicle into individual sections – chambers (Fig.2), in which appropriately-shaped gas bags will be folded up, inserted and then filled with gas." This point was accompanied by a clarifying sentence: "This arrangement, which however is not part of the existing invention, but instead is protected by Patent No.91887." This patent did not belong to Graf Zeppelin.[19]

LZ 1 Is Built

The airship of David Schwarz, who died during its construction, had been financed by Carl Berg alone. After the failure of its one and only flight in November 1897, he therefore gladly grabbed the chance to become involved in another aviation project offered him by Graf Zeppelin. In this way Zeppelin enjoyed the benefits of the experience Berg had gained with the Schwarz airship. Their business relationship was very good, but not entirely free of tension. Carl Berg Jr. described it very idealistically: "In fact, very rarely had there ever been such a frictionless collaboration as between these two men in the heated efforts to benefit the Fatherland and help make one of mankind's oldest dreams a reality. This collaboration lasted from autumn 1897 until Berg's untimely death on 26 May 1906. While on his deathbed, he instructed his heirs not to abandon the count. Zeppelin always acknowledged the great part Berg had played in his businesses."[20]

Carl Berg received the contract to make the aluminum parts for the airship frame, after a contract to deliver aluminum for air vehicles exclusively to Schwarz had been replaced. Manufacture of the framework components began in Lüdenscheid in autumn 1898. Before

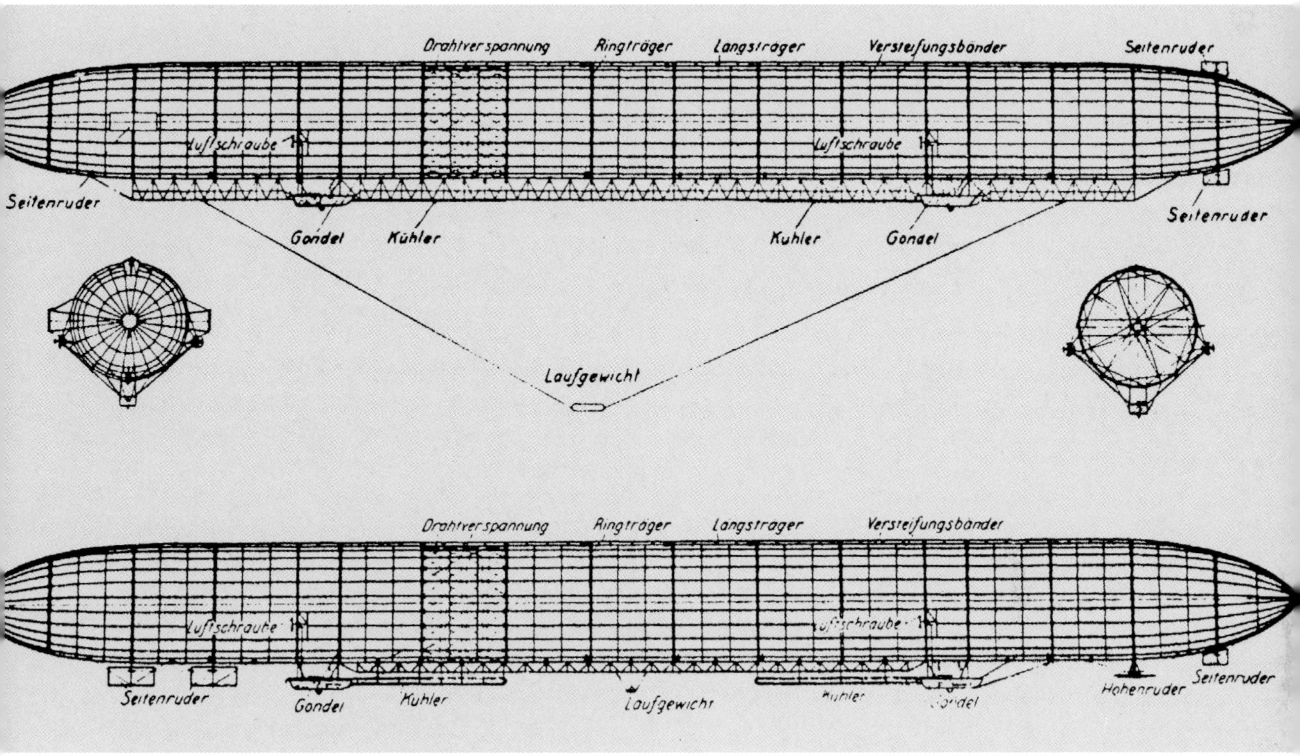

Schematic drawing of LZ 1. The upper version represents the airship at the time of its first ascent in July 1900, while the lower version depicts the airship after conversion prior to its 2nd and 3rd flights in October 1900 (later drawings by Dürr, 1936).

being sent, the supporting parts were test-fitted on rings and fuselage segments. A hangar was required for assembly of the airship in Friedrichshafen, for the huge and extremely light body of the airship had to be protected from the wind and weather. The idea to build a floating hangar on Lake Constance seemed brilliant. It was only anchored at its fully closed end and thus could turn by itself in the wind. The airship sat inside the hangar on a raft, which could exit and enter with or against the wind and was thus relatively safe from dangerous cross winds. The frequently rough weather of Lake Constance often threatened the hangar, however, and on one occasion it even broke free and had to be retrieved by a steamer. Assembly inside the hangar was not always simple, because the movement of the waves was transmitted by the raft to the airship. To mitigate the movements, the float was later suspended from the hangar roof with blocks and tackles. Photographs, in which considerable deformation of the girders may be seen, document the lack of experience in assembling the framework, but also shortcomings of the design. Anther cause for this was the low strength of the aluminum. Carl Berg worked intensively on better alloys.

One of the outstanding personalities produced by Luftschiffbau Zeppelin was Ludwig Dürr.[21] He took part in the creation of all of the Zeppelin airships and, with the exception of LZ 1, oversaw the construction of every Zeppelin. His descriptions in the "Magazine of the Zeppelin Companies" gives a good impression of the building of LZ 1.[22]

Ludwig Dürr: "About the Building of the First Zeppelin Airship"

"… A cylinder with a diameter of 11.6 meters and a length of ninety-six meters was chosen as the lifting body, to which were attached a nose and tail, each sixteen meters long. Its shape was patterned after projectile points. The body was divided into fifteen sections of eight meters and two sections above the gondolas of four meters

Ludwig Dürr.

length, so that the balloon's total volume of 11,300m³ was divided by braced rings into seventeen sections. The shape of the body was a 24-corner, formed by rings, at the corners of which the I-shaped girders, cross-linked with brackets, ran the entire length to the tips of the nose and tail. These were themselves butt-joined to the ring corners and connected with angled joint plates and rivets. Bracing of the rings was achieved by radial cables and sinew rope overlapping three corners, the former made of steel, the latter aluminum wire rope. The longitudinal bearer boxes were tensioned with diagonal wires for longitudinal stiffness. As well, on the perimeter in each section two aluminum bands were fastened to the girders, which were not placed under tension, however, until under gas pressure. The gas area was fitted with ramie cord mesh attached to the inner belt of the beams, to create the cells and maintain an airspace between the cells and the outer shell.

A catwalk made of aluminum sections and perforated metal, the length of the cylindrical part of the ship, was suspended by wires from the lowest field, allowing the entire body of the ship to be inspected. The parts of the catwalk forward of the forward gondola and aft of the rear gondola served as a track for a sliding 150kg weight, which, when required, could be suspended by a winch from the gondola, in order to shift the center of gravity fore and aft.

The power plants were housed in two nacelles made of aluminum sheet over frames. These are supposed to be suspended from the framework on aluminum tubes and wires. By means of a reversing gear and tubular shafts, the gasoline engine in each gondola drove the propellers, which were installed in tubular

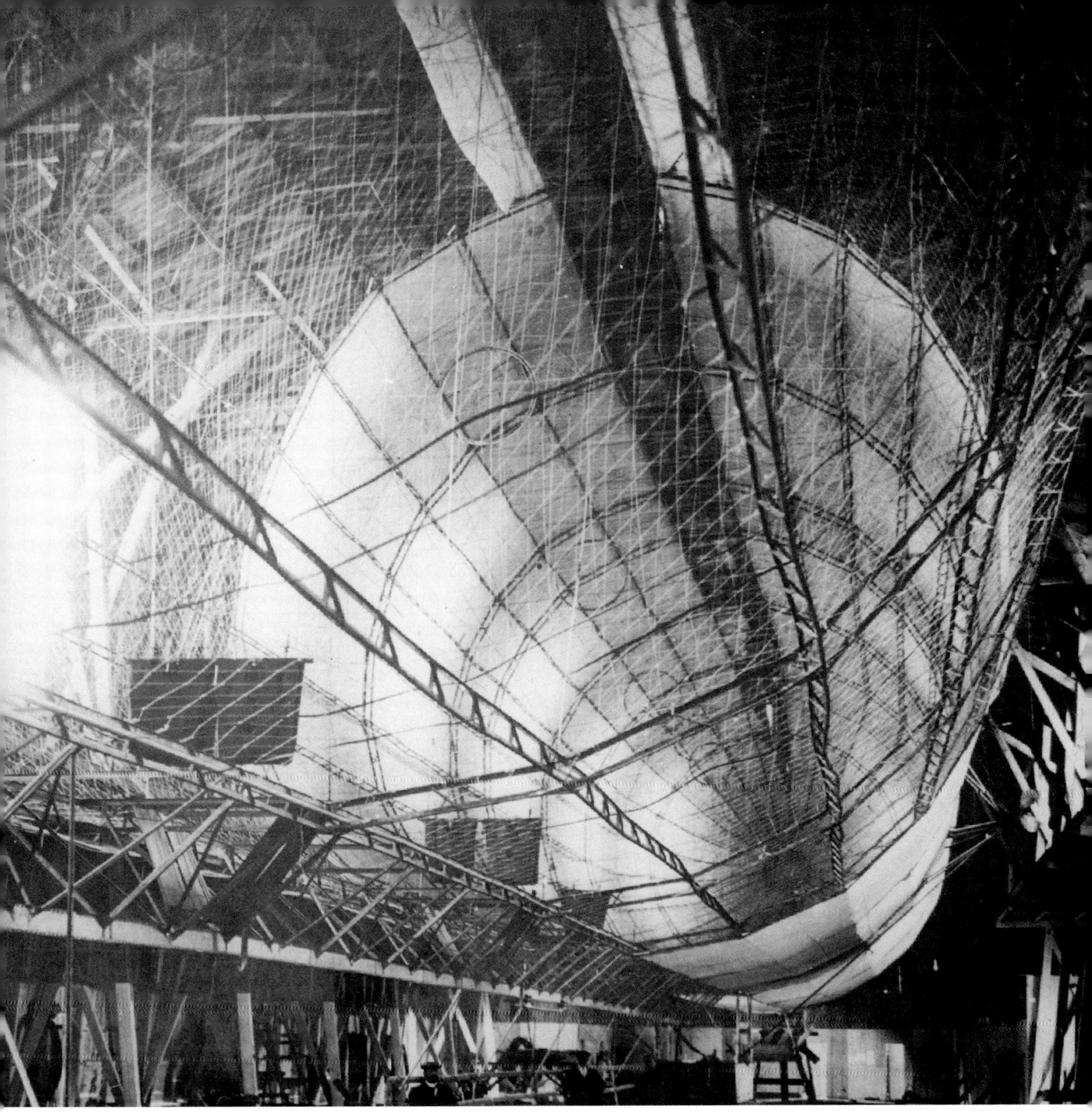

The framework of LZ 1 with partially applied shell. The girders, which were only two-dimensional, are quite bent in places.

mounts on top to the side, in the calculated drag center plane. Re-cooling of the engine cooling water took place in ribbed pipes suspended from the catwalk. The cooling surface of the ribs was $27m^2$ for each engine. The gasoline was housed in a tank in each nacelle. Gasoline was delivered to the engine by means of exhaust gas pressure.

The ship was controlled and steered from the forward gondola. A lever operated the rudder control, a winch controlled movement of the sliding weight, there was an engine telegraph for the aft gondola, a board for the valve and ballast slides, plus a table for maps and the barographs, a fluid level and a pendulum for reading changes in pitch.

To accommodate the gas, each of the seventeen sections had a cell of rubberized cotton, which with 60g rubber coating weighed $150g/m^2$. All cells had lugs for lifting and seats for the overpressure and maneuvering valves. Of the latter, three were arranged in the ship center and one each in the first and last

Daimler engines for LZ 1; in the foreground reverse gear unit and drive shafts.

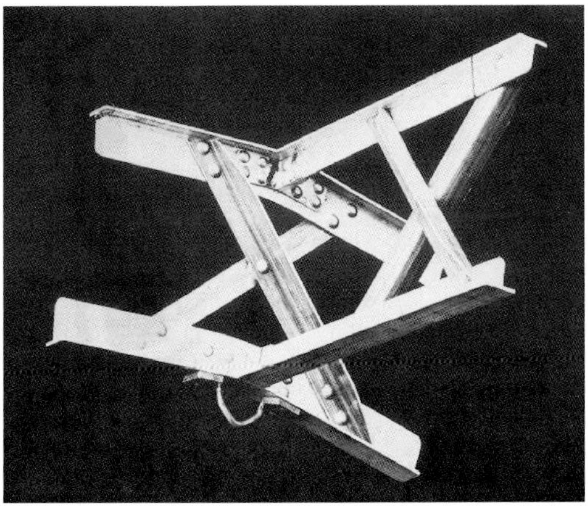

Junction from the framework of LZ 1.

cylindrical cells. The valves were operated by wires, which were housed in aluminum tubes between the front and rear walls to the lower girder field and to the control gondola, and which after activation were closed by spring balancers. The overpressure valves consisted of a rubber membrane which lay against a plate. The gas could escape with just a few millimeters of excess pressure.

The outer skin of the lifting body consisted of waterproof impregnated cotton fabric called Pegamoid in the upper part, which was sewn together and attached by eyelets and cords to the girders, and by eyelets and buttons (studs) to the rings. In the first field slots were installed on the rings. Overlaid with cloth material, they enabled ventilation of the inner area and gas discharge and nevertheless kept out the rain. The lower half was covered with impregnated silk weighing 48g/m^2. Between the outer shell and the gas cells was an air space of 18cm for ventilation and insulation against sunbeams.

For steering of the ship, there were two trapezoid-shaped control surfaces on the bow, one above and one below, pivoting in their center planes, while rectangular control surfaces, each with an area of 4.5m^2, were installed on the rear end of the cylindrical part at the mid point. The controls could be operated from the driver's cabin by control wires, all simultaneously or, by unhooking, individually, whereby the disabled surfaces could be locked in the neutral position. Fabric bags, suspended from the rings, were arranged for the carriage of water ballast. Two bags, each with a content of 250kg, could, by draining a swiveling discharge pipe installed in the bags, be emptied to the extent desired, while twelve bags each with a content of fifty liters could be emptied instantaneously by releasing a hose. Total ballast capacity was 1,250kg.

Thirty-meter-long ropes were attached on the sides of each ring for handling the airship during ascent and landing. The ropes were different colors meter by meter, which was supposed to permit an even raising of the airship on command. Then a rope was provided on the forward gondola for towing on the water. Each gondola had a bumper wheel, mounted in a track, with a shock absorber to absorb the impact, for possible landings on solid ground, while for water landings the rounded bottoms of the gondolas acted as shock absorbers.

LZ 1 is released; below on the raft the ground handling crew, left the steamboat for towing the raft out of the hangar.

The heart of the ship, the engines, were then still in the initial stages, very robust and massive, therefore with a weight of 385kg and a measured output of 12.3 HP [9.0 kW] at the propeller shaft they could hardly be called 'airship engines.'"

The Ascents of LZ 1

Considerable difficulties were encountered with the gas cells. They leaked. Months passed before a suitable sealing material, called Ballonin, a rubber solution developed by the Finnish airship maker Lievendahl, was found. The first ascent was planned for autumn 1899, however this could not be made because of problems with the gas cells. This resulted in unpleasant financial problems, for the company's funds for promoting airship travel had been used up. To save the group, a guarantee fund of at least 150,000 Marks was required. Graf Zeppelin subscribed 50,000 and Carl Berg 25,000 Marks, but by 4 April 1900 just 88,730 Marks had been raised, and Zeppelin saw himself forced to also sign for the remaining 61,270 Marks. Several bad storms, one of which caused one of the floating hangar's pontoons to spring a leak, caused further commotion.

On 30 June the long-awaited filling of the gas cells with 11,000m³ of hydrogen gas, which was compressed in 2,600 cylinders, took place. The filling process, which went according to plan, was rated a master technical achievement. It had to take place so that the seventeen lifting cells were filled as evenly as possible, which required a considerable technical effort – for pontoons to transport the many gas cylinders and for the complicated system of pipes, hoses and valves. The flight planned for the next day could not be made, however, because many details had to be improved and tested. Inspection of the filled gas cells, in particular, took more time than forecast, consequently in the evening the ship was only moved out of and back into the hangar.

The first ascent took place at about 20:00 on 2 July 1900. Wind with a speed of approximately 7m/sec had prevented an earlier ascent, for it had been agreed that wind speed could not be more than 4m/sec for the first ascent. In the command gondola were Graf Zeppelin, Baron Konrad von Bassus[23] and Fritz Burr, an engineer; in the aft gondola were machinist Groß plus the journalist Eugen Wolf of the newspaper *Die Woche* from the Berlin publishing company owned by August Scherl, who had always been well-disposed towards

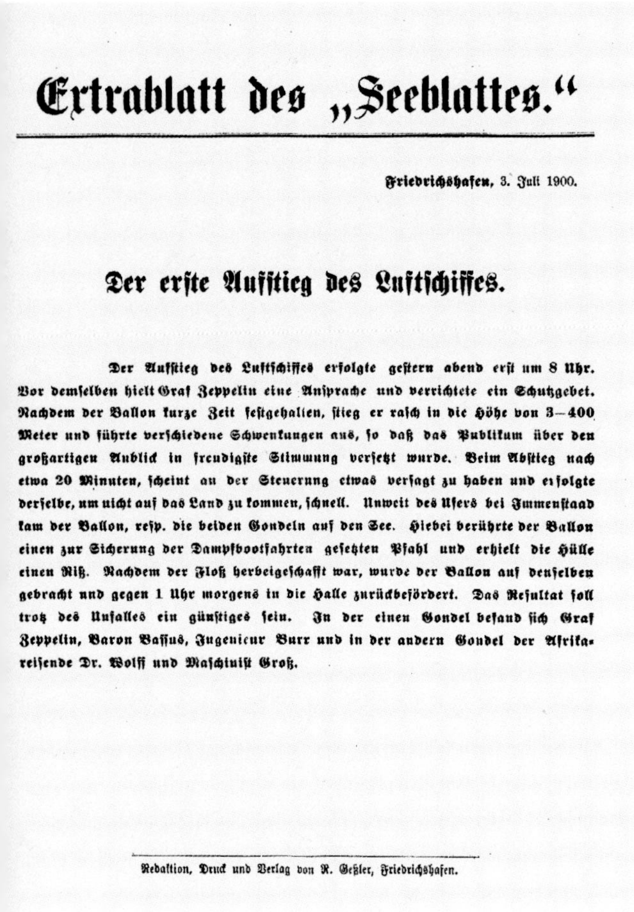

Extrablatt des „Seeblattes."

Friedrichshafen, 3. Juli 1900.

Der erste Aufstieg des Luftschiffes.

Der Aufstieg des Luftschiffes erfolgte gestern abend erst um 8 Uhr. Vor demselben hielt Graf Zeppelin eine Ansprache und verrichtete ein Schutzgebet. Nachdem der Ballon kurze Zeit festgehalten, stieg er rasch in die Höhe von 3–400 Meter und führte verschiedene Schwenkungen aus, so daß das Publikum über den großartigen Anblick in freudigste Stimmung versetzt wurde. Beim Abstieg nach etwa 20 Minuten, scheint an der Steuerung etwas versagt zu haben und erfolgte derselbe, um nicht auf das Land zu kommen, schnell. Unweit des Ufers bei Immenstaad kam der Ballon, resp. die beiden Gondeln auf den See. Hiebei berührte der Ballon einen zur Sicherung der Dampfbootfahrten gesetzten Pfahl und erhielt die Hülle einen Riß. Nachdem der Floß herbeigeschafft war, wurde der Ballon auf denselben gebracht und gegen 1 Uhr morgens in die Halle zurückbefördert. Das Resultat soll trotz des Unfalles ein günstiges sein. In der einen Gondel befand sich Graf Zeppelin, Baron Bassus, Ingenieur Burr und in der andern Gondel der Afrikareisende Dr. Wolff und Maschinist Groß.

Redaktion, Druck und Verlag von R. Geßler, Friedrichshafen.

Special edition of the newspaper Seeblatt covering the first ascent by LZ 1, Friedrichshafen, from 3 July 1900.

the count. *Hauptmann* Hermann Moedebeck[24] had come to Lake Constance as an observer. He wrote about the ascent in the *Ilustrierte Aeronautische Mitteilungen*:[25] "… The raft was brought out at 7:30 in the evening; at 07:50 it was south of the balloon hangar facing into the wing. They were tense moments, with sharp-sounding commands from an airship officer 'one meter higher!' finally followed by 'release!' coming one after another in rapid succession. At 8:30 in the evening the airship was free. Nose-first, the vehicle rose slowly and, after the aft and then the forward engines were started, immediately turned itself into the wind in almost completely level flight. Soon afterwards one saw that Graf Zeppelin had turned the forward control surface to the right, the rear to the left. The airship immediately responded to this control position, completing a turn to the right. After completing this, it again positioned itself with the sternpost into the wind and the nose dropped, the sliding weight appeared to have moved forward. Several minutes later the machine stopped; the airship drifted with the wind with light oscillations about the longitudinal axis, while twice turning about its vertical axis before it gently touched down on Lake Constance close to the steamer jetty near Immenstadt. As it did so its engines were used repeatedly, briefly forwards, briefly backwards, but always in the direction of the lake. Graf von Zeppelin gave the signal that he intended to land at 8:15, the landing itself was completed at 8:20 in the evening." Hermann Moedebeck completed his account with the encouraging sentence: "The completed task, keeping a, by our present standards, enormously large airship of rigid design with a gas volume of 11,000m^3 with safe gasoline engines stable in the air and landing on the surface of the water without damage, is itself an awe-inspiring achievement. But we demand much more; in this test we see only the first tentative step and call to all who took part: 'Onwards!'"

Many other correspondents also reported on the first experimental flight, among them of course Eugen Wolf, who had been aboard the airship and who had become famous because of stories about his extended trips to Africa. Graf Zeppelin had arranged for Wolf to take part in the first ascent for good reason. Wolf, who had once been an intimate of Bismarck,[26] was a friend of Hermann von Wissmann, the former African explorer and governor of German East Africa.[27] His contacts among the various colonial associations and societies, like the Society for German Colonization, the Society for the Evangelical-Lutheran Mission in East Africa, and the German Colonial Society, were as important to the count as the military on account of the expected support for the airship from that direction.

Graf Zeppelin Speaks

It is interesting the Zeppelin himself took part in the first test flight. Written in the name

Boys watch the first ascent.

of the Society for the Promotion of Airship Travel,[28] his account, which had to sound as positive as possible for the previously bitterly-disappointed shareholders of the society, gave an good overall assessment of the flight but then went on to address various shortcomings: "... Consequently, as it is the design would be a practical vehicle, if it possessed sufficient speed for use in a sufficiently large number of days in the year. This could not be determined from the test that took place. Namely for the following reasons: because two handling ropes on the rear end were held too long, its upwards movement lagged behind during the ascent by the vehicle. As soon as the ropes were released, the sliding weight was moved forward. As a result the vehicle moved back towards the horizontal position and, after achieving same, reached its maximum speed during the flight, as the propellers were by then producing thrust. At that moment it moved forward rapidly against the 5.5m/sec wind that had just come up (measured by the tethered observation balloon). This moment was much too short, however, to allow it to come even close to achieving its true maximum speed. This was because, while attempting to return the sliding weight to the neutral position, the crank for the same broke, and the vehicle immediately adopted a nose-down attitude. There was also a slight torsional moment, caused by a minor bend in the longitudinal axis (about 27cm over a vehicle length of 128m), which because of the broken crank could not be countered with the sliding weight. The imminent danger of rolling over had to be immediately countered by stopping and reversing the propellers. From then on the entire flight consisted of alternately applying forward and reverse thrust with the propellers to stabilize attitude. Another reason for this switching process arose from the condition that the vehicle, which initially responded well to rudder inputs to starboard, no longer turned to the left, because of a slight indentation on the port side, probably caused by the jamming of the sliding weight, which acted as a control surface. Also for this reason, if the aft end was facing the lake, the propellers had to be reversed to avoid being carried over land. There is no doubt that the obstacles in determining speed that developed on this first test flight (broken crank, slight bends, etc.) can be avoided for the next test. In particular, we envisage moving the mounting for the sliding weight more towards the center and a powerful strengthening of the bottom girders between the two gondolas. As the low-hanging sliding weight is uncomfortable during ascent and landing, it will now hang down only as far as the bottoms of the gondolas. It is possible that the vehicle will now demonstrate inadequate longitudinal stability. In this case, during subsequent tests the sliding weight will again have to be arranged lower and with more widely-spaced attachment points, or another system to address the problem will have to be found."

Improvements Are Made

After the first ascent a number of improvements were carried out on the airship. These included modification of the catwalk, which was given a triangular covered keel framework instead of the suspended walkway, in order to stiffen the entire structure. As demanded by Zeppelin in his report, the sliding weight now hung so that it did not project beyond the bottom of the gondola. The upper rudder on the nose was done away with, while the two tail controls on the sides were removed and arranged in tandem beneath the ship's fuselage, giving them freedom of movement. An elevator forward of the pilot's gondola was supposed to assist the efforts of the sliding weight. The ballast water controls were improved and damaged fairings were replaced with stronger material. But before the next test flight could be made, there was an accident. Already filled with fuel and ballast, on 24 September 1900 the ship crashed onto the hangar floor because of a broken suspension mount. It was so badly damaged that repairs initially seemed hopeless, nevertheless on 17 October the airship was able to undertake its second flight, watched by the King of Wurttemberg. It lasted one hour and twenty minutes. The ship supposedly achieved a speed of 8m/sec (28.8kph). The controls did not perform as well as expected. The failure of a valve led to the emptying of one of the forward gas cells and resulted in a rather heavy landing, which had no serious consequences however. A third and last ascent followed on 21 October, but it lasted just twenty-three minutes. The empty lifting gas cell had to be filled with lower-quality gas, consequently, only 30kg of ballast could be carried in order to have at least 20kg of lift. As a result, the ship was greatly lightened in the center and bulged upwards noticeably, preventing the propeller axes from working horizontally. Consequently, as on the first flight, the nose dropped during forward flight, the tail during backwards flight.[29]

After this flight, there was no money with which to fill the cells with the necessary high-quality gas. The guarantee funds of 150,000 Marks and a donation of 11,000 Marks from the Prince of Hohenlohe-Öhringen were used up and no new funds were flowing into the company. On 15 November 1900, it was decided by the general assembly of the Company for the Promotion of Airship Travel, to dissolve and liquidate the company.

Airships prior to the First World War

The sad chapter of the liquidation of the Company for the Promotion of Airship Travel came to an end on 28 February 1902. Graf Zeppelin did not allow himself to be thrown off track, however, and never gave up his vision of the rigid airship. In a letter written to him by Melanie Schwarz, the widow of airship builder David Schwarz, on 29 December 1900, there is a defiant handwritten note that exudes unbroken optimism: "Noon 1/1/01. Reply – start again. Z."[30]

It Will Definitely Go On

The count had thus made the decision to build another airship. It was completely uncertain how this was to happen. Bankruptcy was a bitter blow for the shareholders, and convincing them to contribute again was hopeless. Zeppelin therefore needed to find new shareholders. As well, the critics now had their second wind. The experiment had cost at least one-million Marks and no forwards-looking result was in sight. It also benefited him little when Kaiser Wilhelm II unexpectedly awarded him the Order of the Red Eagle First Class on 7 January 1901[31] and expressed optimism in the award document: "The results achieved signify an epoch-making advance in the construction of airships and have created a valuable basis for further experiments with existing materials. I will afford my assistance to such experiments by making the advice and experience of the airship department available to you at all times. I have therefore ordered that the airship department shall send an officer to your subsequent tests whenever required." For Zeppelin could expect little in the way of help directly from the airship department. After the failed attempt by the Schwarz airship and the modest results with Zeppelin's LZ 1, the military, including some former advocates, declared the rigid system unsuitable for military purposes and instead bolstered its support for the non-rigid or semi-rigid systems. With these "balloons" the units would be more mobile, require no hangars and also be cheaper, arguments the count soon found himself forced to counter. And had the Frenchmen Renard and Krebs not proved years ago that it was possible to fly specific courses, of which Zeppelin so far could only dream, with non-rigid airships? In Germany names like August von Parseval[32] and Nikolaus Basenach[33] soon appeared, eager to prove that the military point of view was correct. No matter what the Kaiser might have thought would result from his decree: after the liquidation of the company, the count lacked money, any broad basis for business activities and support from the military. The VDI tried to portray Zeppelin's experiments accurately and correctly, but there were too many voices in the association speaking out against the rigid system. A derogatory statement by von Lossow, a member of the VDI's board, urging caution is typical: "For the time being, my personal feeling is that if large sums became available to the count as a result of moral support from the Association of German Engineers, the resulting advances and results would correspond just as little to the capital expended as before."[34]

With no hope of obtaining funding for a new airship and for the continuation of flight trials, in June 1901 Zeppelin decided to scrap LZ 1 and abandon needed repairs on the floating hangar. What remained was the hope that with an intensive effort to convince the skeptics, he might yet be able to turn the ship around.

The Creation of LZ 2 and LZ 3

Of Zeppelin's former colleagues, a handful remained active, among them Ludwig Dürr. He dedicated himself to improving the airship, in particular the stability of the lifting body structure. The use of longitudinal and ring girders with triangular cross-sections, with which Dürr experimented and achieved good results, was to result in a decisive advance in future airships. As a letter from Dürr reveals, the count himself inspired these beam variants.[35]

As time passed without prospects of obtaining funding for the construction of a new airship, Graf Zeppelin turned to methods that can be characterized as tragic. In the summer of 1903, to a selected circle of about 8,000 members of the "educated classes" he sent out an "appeal to the German people" together with postal order forms, however the resulting donations barely covered half of his personal costs of the action. In October 1903, as a last resort, a "distress call to save airship travel" appeared in the newspapers *Die Woche*, *Der Tag* and the *Berliner Lokal-Anzeiger*. This, too, achieved little, as not even 15,000 Marks came in despite the imploring final sentence: "There is an urgent need for those of you who want to have airship travel to offer the means that you alone can provide. Hurry! Otherwise you will not be able to seize the gem sinking into the depths!"

In the end, however, Zeppelin's persistence paid off. A lottery authorized by the Württembergian royal family brought in about 130,000 Marks, and even the Reich chancellor made available 50,000 Marks from his contingency fund. The Daimler Company declared itself ready to provide engines for a new airship free of charge, and because of old ties Carl Berg offered to provide the aluminum parts at no cost. Other potential suppliers made similar offers. Under these conditions, it was not all that difficult for the count to decide to invest more of his own assets in the matter, and in April 1905 he was able to begin construction of LZ 2. It soon turned out, however, that he had underestimated the construction costs by 365,000 Marks, especially as the cost of a new hangar had to be factored in.

Preparations for the construction of LZ 2 may be seen as very thorough. Not only had Ludwig Dürr experimented with the new triangular beams, and worked closely with Carl Berg to develop stronger alloys, he had also worked just as hard on producing better materials for the lifting gas cells, tested engines and experimented with the propellers to improve their effectiveness. A propeller-driven boat was used for this purpose on Lake Constance. Beginning in 1904, Dürr, who prior to this had carried out almost all of the important development work alone, received assistance from a mechanical engineer from the Daimler-Motorenbau-Gesellschaft. Like LZ 1, the new airship was 128 meters long and had a diameter of 11.65 meters; the two engines were significantly more powerful and each produced 85 HP (62.5 kW).

LZ 2 in front of the floating hangar on Lake Constance.

Of course the old problem soon reared its head once again: the financing. According to a balance sheet drawn up at the end of 1905, the income from the lottery, subsidy from the Reich Chancellor, donations, contributions from the count, interest income, etc was 285,000 Marks, against expenses of no less than 470,000 Marks, and Graf Zeppelin was again forced to bridge the financing gap. But as it was hoped that the ship could be sold to the military for 1.5 million Marks, which would have been enough to cover even old cost burdens, Zeppelin urged haste and on 30 November 1905 dared a takeoff attempt, even though the weather was not exactly favorable that day. When the ship cast off from the tug, the rope became entangled and pulled the nose down, while the tail rose above the surface of the water. When the aft engine was started – the forward engine refused to start – the nose was driven into the water so forcefully that the forward elevator was destroyed. Then, as the airship was being towed back to the hangar, the forward rudder was torn off.

By the time repairs had been completed, the gas fill had become unusable, and the next test flight had to be put off until 16 January 1906. At altitude LZ 2 became caught in a wind current. After the failure of one engine and partial failure of the control system, the crew was forced to put the airship down near Sommersried between Kisslegg and Wangen in the Allgäu. The landing was trouble-free, but the anchor was unable to get a grip in the frozen ground. The airship was carried by the wind and sustained such damage that there was no other choice but to scrap it, just 35km from its home port as the crow flies.

LZ 2 received little attention from writers. Wolfgang Meighörner-Schardt declared: "Often the direct successor of an epochal invention stands in the shadow of the first born, and its secondary quality is often only recognized by experts. This is particularly applicable to the Zeppelin airship LZ 2, in whose case several

LZ 3 over Lake Constance in the summer of 1907.

LZ 3's first ascent from the mainland on 16 March 1909. Note the absence of port elevator controls.

factors have combined to prevent an adequate accounting until now. First, there was no longer the character of a sensation, LZ 1 had earned this glory for itself on 2 July 1900. Secondly, in the case of LZ 2 Graf Zeppelin's information policy was more restrained, probably because of his bitter experiences after LZ 1's first ascent. But finally – and this may be the main reason for the lack of attention paid to LZ 2 – the airship was truly not under a lucky star."[36]

Despite the debacle of LZ 2, Zeppelin still believed that he should build another airship, and the main issue was again the financing, which he initially tried to resolve through Carl Berg in Lüdenscheid and the Prussian war minister Karl Wilhelm von Einem.[37] Faced with recent experience, however, both declined. Zeppelin was nevertheless able to convince

Crown Prince Wilhelm of Prussia in the command gondola of LZ 3 (in the center) on 7 August 1908.

LZ 3 back in service on 23 October 1908 after modifications.

the government offices in Berlin and the Württembergian royal house that the accident in Kisslegg had not been attributable to the system, but to a combination of unforeseeable factors. In the end two new lotteries were authorized and these earned enough money to build airship LZ 3 using the salvageable parts from LZ 2. The new airship was able to make its maiden flight on 9 October 1906. It had the same external dimensions as its two predecessors. Unlike them, however, it had stabilizing surfaces on the tail. LZ 3 logged 4398km in forty-five flights before it was taken over by the army with the designation Z I. These included an eight-hour flight with twenty-five persons on board, which caused the previously mentioned formation of the DELAG. LZ 3 was ultimately lengthened to 136 meters, resulting in a 900m^3 increase in lifting gas volume to 12,200m^3. It was also fitted with two 105 HP (77 kW) engines [later 115 HP, 84.5 kW]. It served well as a training ship and was finally scrapped in March 1913, because it had become obsolescent.

LZ 4 Makes the Breakthrough despite Catastrophe

LZ 3 had also convinced the government of the Reich, which authorized 500,000 Marks for Zeppelin to continue his experiments. New lotteries brought in more money, and the army department let it be known that it would pay 3.05 million Marks for two more airships. Thus all of the money worries of the Luftschiffbau in Friedrichshafen were gone. But first a twenty-four-hour endurance flight had to be completed to demonstrate the performance of the Zeppelin airships. This requirement had been raised in late-1906 during meetings with government authorities[38] and was subsequently confirmed, by the Inspectorate of Transportation Units among others.[39]

The construction of LZ 4 began in the hangar on the shore of Lake Constance in late 1907. At the same time a new hangar was built on the lake using government funds, the so-called "Reich floating hangar." The larger hangar made it possible to increase LZ 4's diameter by thirteen meters. Gas volume was

LZ 4 with fore and aft rudder controls, an arrangement that failed to prove itself.

15,000m^3, and the two Daimler engines each produced 105 HP (77 kW). For the first time, a small passenger cabin was installed on the walkway. The first flight took place on 20 June 1908. Several modifications were soon made, including to the steering controls. One of the most prominent changes was a large rudder on the tail. The control surface in the nose was removed. A twelve-hour flight over Switzerland with twelve persons on board was seen as a good omen for the planned twenty-four-hour endurance flight. Graf Zeppelin was now on everyone's lips and on 8 July 1908, his seventieth birthday, he was showered with honors. The twenty-four -hour endurance flight, scheduled for 4-5 August 1908, was supposed to be the climax of this euphoric period. But the experiment ended in disaster. Mechanical problems forced the airship to make a second unplanned stop in Echterdingen, where the airship was destroyed on the ground by a thunderstorm.

The Accident in Echterdingen

Zeppelin himself wrote extensively about the endurance flight and its end, where in addition to describing the flight, he also provided an insight into flight procedures:[40] "Takeoff was made under favorable conditions. During the twelve-hour Swiss trip, the vehicle had shown that all of its parts functioned as desired. Weather conditions were relatively favorable. I say relatively, because in high summer there are considerable temperature differences between day and night. The ship would sail from the night coolness into the heat of the day,

LZ 4 after modification, with large aft rudder, auxiliary rudders between the horizontal stabilizers, and upper and lower vertical stabilizers.

and the coolness of night would not return until much weight had been lost through the burning of fuel. To the extent that the program went according to plan – it was supposed to reach Mainz in twenty-four hours of uninterrupted flight and cover 700 kilometers – one can say that the receipt was on our bill. But even the part of the flight that was not according to program confirmed the correctness of my assumptions in another respect, namely the two unintended landings. There have always been doubts that a rigid airship like this could be landed on solid ground with complete safety as it is on water. The landing at the selected place

LZ 4 emerges from the hangar for its twenty-four-hour endurance flight; the flight had received a great deal of publicity and drew many people to Lake Constance.

in Echterdingen was so smooth that those in the gondola could scarcely tell it had touched down. If the program was interrupted by two unintended landings, one must visualize the reasons for them in order to be able to properly judge. Essentially it was this: the arrival of the heat of day and sunlight on the vehicle resulted in increased lift, while at the same time the ballast was sharply reduced because of fuel consumption, which was about sixty kilograms every hour. If one eliminated this lift entirely, it

The end of the endurance flight; after engine trouble forced LZ 4 to land near Echterdingen, it was destroyed by a thunderstorm.

would result in the loss of a great deal of gas, because the gas expanded as altitude increased and air pressure decreased and, when it had no more room in the cells, was vented by the overpressure valves. Later, when temperatures cooled, one descended into the lower levels, the gas was gone and there was no longer sufficient lift. This lift deficit could be overcome by dynamic force, provided the lifting effect of the tilted vehicle or the elevator controls was sufficient. A difference of one degree between the gas temperature and the outside temperature caused an excess or deficit in lift of about sixty kilograms, and as it was very easy to have a temperature difference of fifteen degrees, the difference was about 900 kilograms. It was therefore a significant force that had to be overcome. This succeeded on the Swiss flight and also now, as long as both engines were working. As soon as one engine had to be stopped, for example to top up the gasoline, or to inspect something, or because of some fault, movement was no longer fast enough and then the lift took the vehicle higher until it reached its natural ceiling. Much gas was lost during this ascent. ... When, in the late afternoon, they approached the Rhine near Oppenheim, there was a very rapid cooling of the gas and, as only one engine was running – the other had become unusable due to the failure of a small wheel, whose replacement took too long at the critical moment – the resulting sink could not be countered dynamically. There was no stopping, and they had to descend all the way to the Rhine. The most suitable location was chosen, and the landing was a complete success. Two things had to happen in order to continue the flight; the ship had to be lightened as much as possible and they had to wait for the coolness of night. As soon as both of these happened, the flight was continued. They went back and forth over Mainz until they were again over Mannheim, where the forward engine failed completely. A bearing had melted out, and from then on they were forced to fly on one engine; but they had plenty of fuel, even for a flight much longer than twenty-four hours. The night was very dark, but they were able to orient themselves and fly by the shortest route to their destination. With just one engine, it was again impossible to avoid being carried to very high altitude, as the vehicle steadily lost weight as fuel was consumed. On reaching an altitude of 1,800 meters, gas was released to avoid climbing higher, but enough that they could still descend with the available dynamic force. So the flight continued over Stuttgart, still at a considerable height. Then, south of Stuttgart, in the Fildern area, a clearly stronger air-current made itself felt, and we realized that we could no longer go forwards on the one remaining engine. Instead of moving forwards, we would have moved backwards. We didn't want that, and after going lower to see if there was a less-strong air-current there, we decided to land. To a certain degree that was the case, and it was hoped that we would be able to move forwards again. But there, too, the headwind soon became so strong that we were barely making any headway. That caused us to land again. We planned to continue the flight after repairing the engine with the assistance of the nearby Daimler plant and purchasing more lifting gas from Manzell. It is known that this landing, too, was completed completely smoothly, without the slightest damage to any part of the vehicle. Then disaster struck. A sudden gale came from the side and carried the vehicle away. It made a jump of a kilometer in length. During this leap one of the people in the airship pulled valves to bring the vehicle back to earth more quickly. The anchor, which had been pulled out and was dangling, struck the ground again. It dug in so firmly that not only was a restraint or something in the vehicle torn off, but the iron anchor itself was broken in two parts. Then the vehicle carried on some distance further until it became lodged in a group of trees, already burning. What matters now is to know whether these unfortunate events could have been avoided or not. They most certainly could have. If we had had as much experience as we have today, we would have known how to maintain altitude on one engine and thus avoided the loss of gas, which was needed for the Rhine landing; but if this was lost, even with one engine we would have been able to reach Friedrichshafen before the storm that halted the flight near Echterdingen developed. We did not know about the unequal warming fore and aft and about other moments, whose explanation would take too long here. Such unequal upward forces fore and aft can be more easily dealt with by more liberal shifting of loads in the airship than by moving the sliding

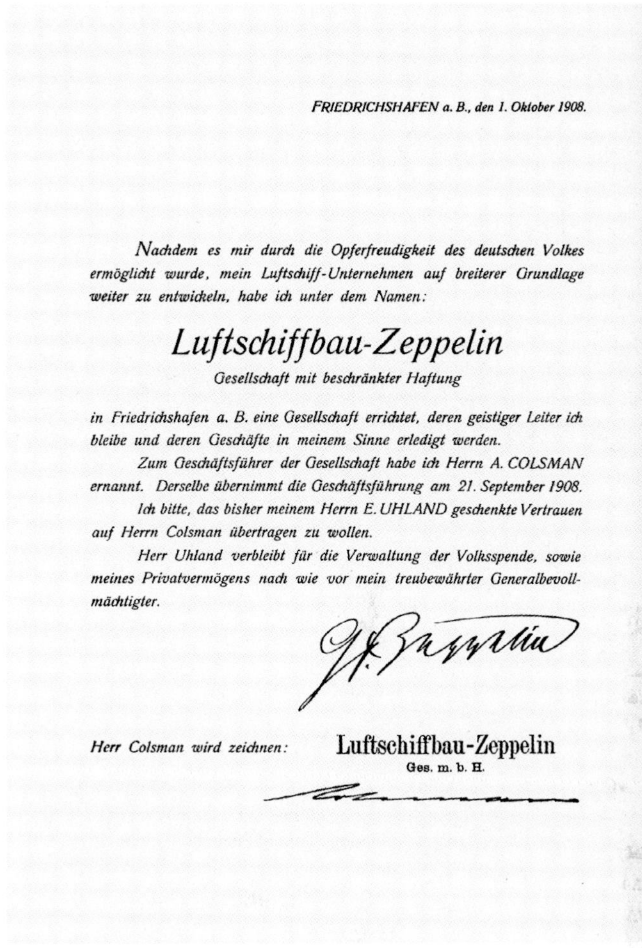

FRIEDRICHSHAFEN a. B., den 1. Oktober 1908.

Nachdem es mir durch die Opferfreudigkeit des deutschen Volkes ermöglicht wurde, mein Luftschiff-Unternehmen auf breiterer Grundlage weiter zu entwickeln, habe ich unter dem Namen:

Luftschiffbau-Zeppelin

Gesellschaft mit beschränkter Haftung

in Friedrichshafen a. B. eine Gesellschaft errichtet, deren geistiger Leiter ich bleibe und deren Geschäfte in meinem Sinne erledigt werden.

Zum Geschäftsführer der Gesellschaft habe ich Herrn A. COLSMAN ernannt. Derselbe übernimmt die Geschäftsführung am 21. September 1908.

Ich bitte, das bisher meinem Herrn E. UHLAND geschenkte Vertrauen auf Herrn Colsman übertragen zu wollen.

Herr Uhland verbleibt für die Verwaltung der Volksspende, sowie meines Privatvermögens nach wie vor mein treubewährter Generalbevollmächtigter.

Herr Colsman wird zeichnen: **Luftschiffbau-Zeppelin** Ges. m. b. H.

Charter of incorporation of the Luftschiffbau Zeppelin GmbH dated 1 October 1908.

weight back and forth. In future, the previously fixed loads, gasoline tanks and the like, will be made easily transportable, making it possible to easily balance any weight differences that are encountered. One method of dealing with excess lift caused by heating and the consumption of fuel statically instead of dynamically, is the taking on of loads during the flight, possibly from water ballast. We already knew that in theory and had tested it over the lake, but we were not experienced enough to use it during the Rhine flight. It is a suitable aid in making long flights, but definitely not a necessity; everything can be accomplished with dynamic means. Why one engine suffered from the effect has not been explained. They suspect that it was caused by the tilted attitude of the vehicle, as a result of which the bearing received less lubrication. That was hardly the case, however; for the airship maintained a largely horizontal attitude during the preceding segment from Oppenheim over Mainz to Mannheim. ... Now, the reason why the vehicle broke free from its mooring near Echterdingen. The mooring equipment on board was on the whole very ample; there were two chain anchors, including a number of augers, the necessary ropes and steel cables etc. But after the landing by the Rhine we had to leave everything unnecessary behind. There was therefore, if I may express it thus, only one set of such equipment available, but even this would have been sufficient to hold the vehicle against a storm directed more against the nose. It wasn't in fact a rope that broke, rather the airship got loose the way it did because, positioned as it was on account of the spectators, the wind from the side raised it up from below and, just as a ship must be directly over its anchor before it comes free, its anchor was pulled out of the ground and carried off. The upward impetus was so great that the crews in the two gondolas, some of whom stayed with the airship – there were about twenty men – were not able to overcome it. This is something else that will unlikely ever be repeated. I am firmly convinced that, if we prevent a gust from blowing under the ship from the side, it can be restrained in any circumstances. One could say: it was reckless to even undertake such flights with so little experience. I must concede that entirely. There were a number of questions that we hadn't yet answered practically. But I was pressed by the situation. My resources were exhausted; in order to continue, I had to get my vehicles inspected and approved as soon as possible, the available one and the damaged one; also to free up space to build more."

Zeppelin's frankness in discussing the problems during the flight and after the forced landing is amazing, but he said nothing about whether the airship would have been able to return to Friedrichshafen even if it had been possible to repair the engine. The ship had vented a great deal of gas in order to be able to land. Where would he get the gas and the equipment for filling the gas cells in the Filder Hills? After the landing near Oppenheim they had simply left behind all non-essential items of equipment and thus made it possible to take off again. At Echterdingen, therefore, much non-essential equipment was probably no longer on board. In any case they had to hurry, for the handlers could not maintain control of the airship, as was shown to be the case.

Effervescent Popularity

As we know, the accident at Echterdingen was a stroke of luck and was the salvation of the Friedrichshafen airship company. In a short time, donations from clubs, industry and members of all classes of society brought in more than six-million Marks, a huge sum in those days. The myth of the "public donations" was born and ultimately made the count one of the most popular men in Germany.

The military, for whom the demonstration flight had actually been made, saw the accident quite differently, however. "Even without the accident ... we can hardly speak about a successful flight. The ship could not have reached the starting point of its flight on its own power," declared a "Statement by the General War Department on the Destruction of the LZ 4." Contrary to Zeppelin's statements, they had "supposed that the ship was capable of a performance ... that it did not possess."[41] But, in their "Zeppelin frenzy," the "people" ignored such statements. As at Kisslegg for LZ 2, a memorial stone was erected where LZ 4 had come to grief. It bore the following verse signed by Prof. Dr. Fehleisen:

"He wrestled with the spirits of the air,
victoriously defeated the fierce enemy.
He rose from the flames
even more splendid than before.
To German pride, the warrior proud,
to him the stone is dedicated – Graf Zeppelin!"

An endless number of Zeppelin poems were written, most of which overflowed with patriotic fervor. A certain Hermann Lehrenkrauss stood out among the poets. Among others, he wrote the following verses to be sung to the melody of The Watch on the Rhine:[42]

"Years ago he was ignored,
his cry for help laughed at!
He went down on his knees before God:
'Almighty, never leave me!'
'Be still, my son and carry on your work,
I remain your mighty refuge,
I have sent your shield to the German people,
As protection for the encircled Fatherland.'
And the people's will, its sanctum:
"That you control your assets,
The Graf Zeppelin gift,
Use it entirely as you see fit,
Complete now with skill, free from care with joy,
Your masterpiece,
For the glory of the German people, you noble hero!
Revered, loved by the entire world."

"On the day of the accident in Echterdingen" [!], the fanatical Zeppelin admirer Lehrenkrauss established the first Zeppelin museum in Stuttgart, where "remains of the airship, busts of Zeppelin, a Zeppelin tree, a Zeppelin table, Zeppelin steins etc," could be admired.[43] There was a boom in Zeppelin devotional objects. The count's likeness appeared on pocket watches, ashtrays, harmonicas, pins, breadboxes, beer glasses, butter and shoe polish tins, labels on schnapps bottles, cheese cartons and sausage banderoles. There was Zeppelin bric-a-brac in the form of busts and statues of all sizes, and it could be had as a nutcracker or Uncle Zeppelin doll. Ladies could purchase Zeppelin handkerchiefs, pastry shops outdid each other in making marzipan Zeppelins and his name appeared in department store windows. That he had to do promotions for cigars was reasonable, but the non-smoker Zeppelin also had to help sell cigarettes. From a Frankfurt butcher shop one can still purchase "original Zeppelin sausage with the permission of his Excellency" in the casing or canned. Even those who hadn't sent a donation to Friedrichshafen wanted to profit from the marketing of the name. Clausberg proved that Graf Zeppelin and his colleagues had their hands full approving requests for authorization to use his name, or denying them when the boundaries of good taste had all to clearly been crossed. Everywhere they were involved in trademark disputes, but frequently the airship builders resigned themselves before the wave of flattering, but not always desired affection that sloshed over them.[44] It is not an exaggeration to speak of "Zeppelinism" in this regard. There were, of course, pleasant aspects as well. Graf Zeppelin was awarded several honorary doctorates, and a number of German cities bestowed honorary citizenship upon him.[45] It will come as no surprise that such occasions saw the playing of brisk, self-composed Zeppelin marches, to which German-nationalistic words were sung.

Airships for DELAG, the Army and the Navy

Construction of LZ 5 (Z II) was begun before the end of 1908 and on 26 May of the following year the ship made its first flight. It was similar in size to LZ 4 and was supposed to be taken on strength by the army. On 29 May LZ 5 took off on a flight to Berlin, but the weather was bad and it only got as far as Bitterfeld. After almost thirty-eight hours in the air, during the return flight to Friedrichshafen the airship collided with a pear tree near Göppingen in the Swabian Alps, severely damaging its nose. After makeshift repairs had been made to the nose using roof battens, because of the amount of gas lost, the flight was continued without the forward engine and without the count. During the flight to Cologne for handover to the army, on 31 July 1909 LZ 5 paid a visit to the International Airship Exhibition (ILA) in Frankfurt. After 16 flights in army service, in April 1910 the ship was stranded in a storm near Weilburg and was scrapped. LZ 6 (maiden flight 25/8/1909) was an experimental ship that was inspected by the ILA in September. It had the same dimensions as its two predecessors but was powered by two somewhat more powerful Daimler engines (2x115 HP [107 kW]). Modification work resulted in an increased length of 144 meters, resulting in a gas capacity of 16,000m^3, and an additional Maybach engine (145 HP) was fitted. The

LZ 5 after a collision with a tree in the Swabian Alps. After the forward gas cell was shortened and underwent makeshift repairs, the airship resumed its flight to Friedrichshafen.

LZ 5 on 31 July 1909 after landing at the ILA in Frankfurt; Mayor Adickes (with top hat) welcomes Graf Zeppelin. In the gondola on the left is Alfred Colsman.

shaft drive was replaced by a steel band drive, which proved unsuccessful and caused many headaches. DELAG took delivery of LZ 6 and it made thirty-four flights for the company with a total of 1,100 persons on board, 726 of them paying passengers, before it burned in the hangar in Baden-Oos on 12 September 1909. LZ 7, which was named *Deutschland*, was built for the DELAG. The most obvious external differences were its single stabilizers on the tail. The nose and tail cones were lengthened by two meters compared to its predecessors and diameter was increased to fourteen meters, resulting in a gas volume of 19,300m³. LZ 7 was the first to have an external covering of goldbeater's skin. It was powered by three Daimler engines each producing 120 HP (88 kW). Great hopes were placed in LZ 7, yet it had but a very brief life. Its maiden flight took place on 19 June 1910, and on 26 June it became stranded in the Teutoburg Forest. In any case during that one week the ship had made seven flights, covering 1,035 kilometers and carrying 142 passengers. Construction

LZ 6 in flight over Lake Constance.

of its replacement, LZ 8, began immediately. The airship flew for the first time on 30 March 1911. It was also an unlucky airship, for after twenty-four ascents and just 2,379 kilometers flown, it was forced against the hangar wall in Dusseldorf and had to be scrapped. The 458 persons transported by LZ 8 included a large number of company personnel under training; just 129 were paying passengers.

The DELAG's next airship was LZ 10 *Schwaben*, which entered service in June 1911.

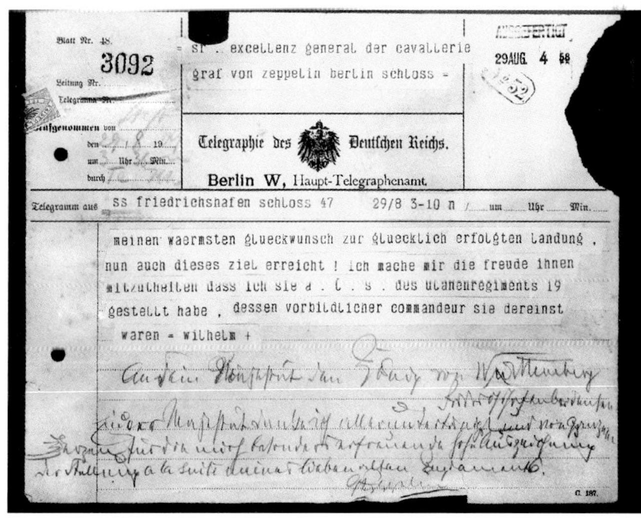

Blatt Nr. 48.
3092
Leitung Nr.
Telegramm Nr.
Aufgenommen von
den 29/8 19
um 3 Uhr 36 Min.
durch

= sr . excellenz general der cavallerie
graf von zeppelin berlin schloss =

Telegraphie des Deutschen Reichs.
Berlin W, Haupt-Telegraphenamt.

29AUG. 4 58

Telegramm aus ss friedrichshafen schloss 47 29/8 3-10 n / um Uhr Min.

meinen waermsten glueckwunsch zur gluecklich erfolgten landung , nun auch dieses ziel erreicht ! ich mache mir die freude ihnen mitzutheilen dass ich sie a . l . s . des ulanenregiments 19 gestellt habe , dessen vorbildlicher commandeur sie dereinst waren = wilhelm +

Telegram from the King of Württemberg to Graf Zeppelin after LZ 6's landing in Berlin on 29 August 1909 with the count's handwritten draft reply.

Daimler engine with an output of 115 hp (84.5 kW) for LZ 6.

With a length of 148 meters, the ship was eight meters shorter than its two predecessors while retaining the same diameter, but it was more powerful, having three Maybach engines each producing 145 HP (107 kW). The *Schwaben* was destroyed by fire in Dusseldorf on 28 June 1912 after 224 flights in which it covered

On 28 August 1909 LZ 6 made a stop in Bitterfeld en route to Berlin.

27,321 kilometers, carrying 1,553 paying passengers out of a total of 4,354 persons transported. During its one year of existence, LZ 10 spent 479 hours in the air. The army airship LZ 9 (replacement for Z II) took off on its maiden flight on 2 October 1911, but immediately afterwards it was modified and enlarged to the dimensions of LZ 10. Because it was obsolescent, LZ 9 was scrapped when the war began. LZ 10 *Schwaben* was still in service when, on 19 February 1912, LZ 11 *Viktoria Luise* made its first flight. It entered passenger service with the DELAG about a month after the *Schwaben* accident, making 489 flights, covering 54,312 kilometers and carrying 9,783 persons, many of them training personnel for the army and navy. The number of paying passengers was 2,295. When war

broke out, LZ 11 served as an army and navy training ship. LZ 11 made its 1,000th flight on 15 June 1915. On 8 October it broke apart while being moved into its hangar. By that time it had flown a total of 1,292 hours, covering 64,125 kilometers and carrying 22,039 persons. Also built for DELAG before the war were LZ 13 *Hansa* (maiden flight 30/7/1912) and LZ 17 *Sachsen* (3/5/1913). Both performed respectably before being taken over by the military when war broke out. LZ 13 made 399 flights in which it flew for 840 hours, covering 44,437 kilometers and carrying 8,321 persons, including 2,187 paying passengers, and LZ 17 made 419 flights, with totals of 39,919 km, 9,837 passengers, 2,465 of them paying, and 741 hours in the air. Both ships were scrapped in 1916. Twelve more ships were completed for

LZ 7 Deutschland takes off on a test flight in June 1910.

LZ 8 Deutschland was placed in service as a replacement for LZ 7.

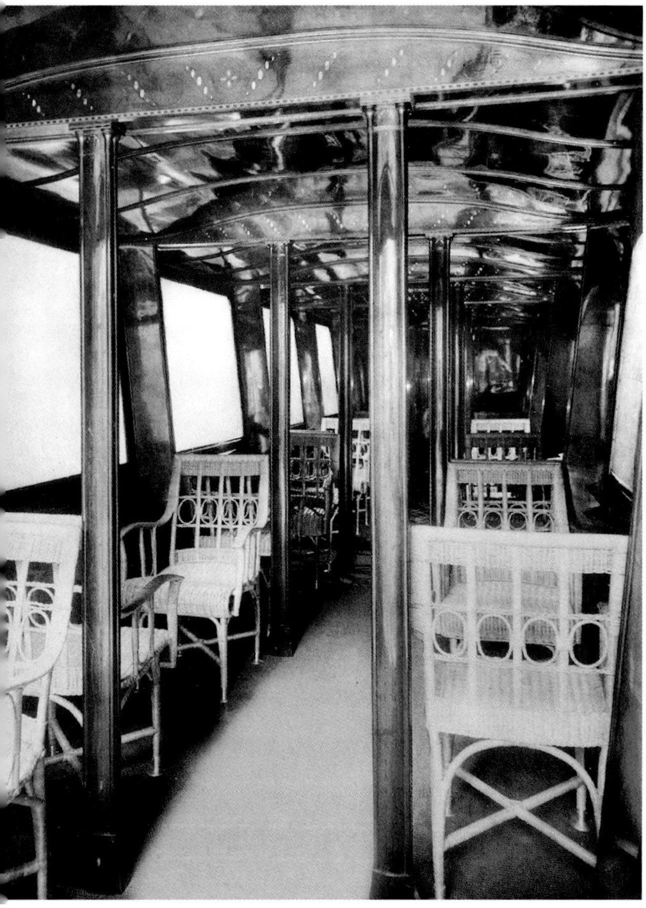

LZ 7's passenger cabin; the internal fittings were largely based on those of railway cars.

LZ 8 broke up while being removed from its hangar in Dusseldorf on 15 November 1911.

LZ 10 Schwaben before a flight with passengers from the Ottoman Empire in 1911.

the army and navy before the outbreak of war: LZ 12 (Z III), LZ 14 (L 1), LZ 15 (replacement Z I), LZ 16 (Z IV), LZ 18 (L 2), LZ 19 (2nd replacement Z I), LZ 20 (Z V), LZ 21 (Z VI), LZ 22 (Z Type VII), LZ 23 (Z VIII), LZ 24 (L 3) and LZ 25 (Z IX). The two navy airships LZ 14 and LZ 18 met especially tragic ends before the start of the war. LZ 14 made its first ascent on 7 October 1912. With a length of 158 meters, a diameter of 14.86 meters and a gas volume of 22,465m³, it was bigger than all previous Zeppelin airships. While on its 74th flight on 9 September 1913, it crashed into the North Sea in a storm and fourteen of its crew of twenty lost their lives. LZ 18 made its maiden flight the same day. Because of its larger 16.6-meter diameter with a gas volume of 27,000m³, this ship was even bigger than LZ 14 and unlike all the other ships for the army and navy before the war, it was equipped with four Maybach engines instead of three, with a combined output of 720 HP (529 kW). While taking off from Berlin-Johannisthal on a training flight on 17 October 1913, LZ 18 caught fire and burned in the air. All twenty-eight persons on board, including civilians, were killed. The two accidents generated fierce reactions from the opponents of the rigid airship system,

LZ 10 Schwaben over the Brandenburg Gate in Berlin.

A film crew poses in airship LZ 13 Hansa for a DELAG advertising photo.

however the military administration stuck with them, which, given the high accident rate among Zeppelin airships, was astonishing. "Graf Zeppelin and his designers gave plausible explanations for the catastrophe in Johannisthal and sharply criticized the military, which had forced through design changes against the will of the Friedrichshafen team. But there was obviously no reason to draw far-reaching conclusions from such accidents."[46] The military also ignored the voices of well-known journalists. For example, the pugnacious Maximilian Harden[47] wrote in his political weekly *Die Zukunft* that the victims of the accidents "had not been sacrificed to the Fatherland, [but] to the idolatry of the monarchy."[48] The LZ 18 catastrophe prompted Victor Silberer, a known balloonist and well-respected author of books on the subject in those years, who favored the semi-rigid airship system, to publish a collection of publications opposing the rigid Zeppelin system,[49] however they had no impact on its supporters.

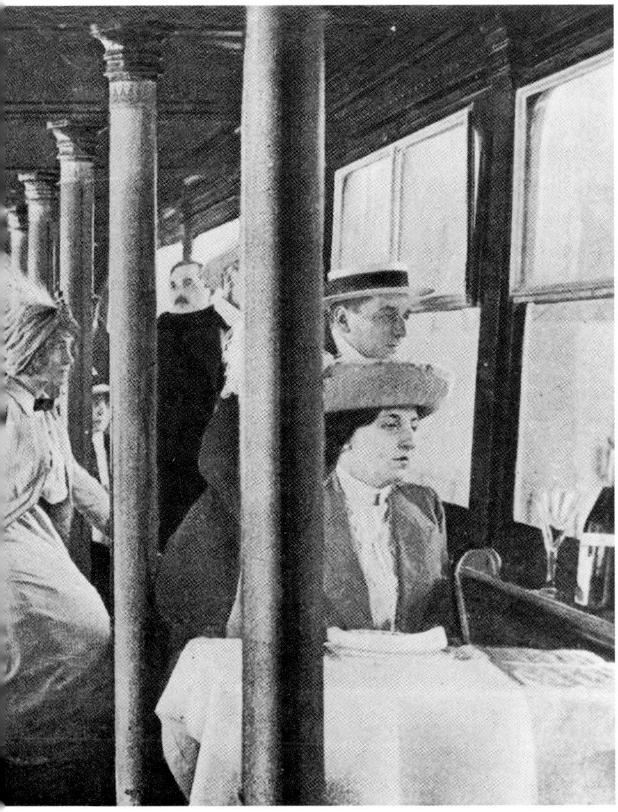

Graf Zeppelin bids farewell to LZ 13 Hansa.

Navy airship L 2 (LZ 18) during its maiden flight on 9 September 1913.

During its delivery flight from Friedrichshafen to Baden-Oos, army airship Z IV (LZ 16) was blown off course and on 3 April 1913 was forced down near Lunéville, France.

The Airship in the First World War

The use of Zeppelin airships in the First World War introduced a new form of warfare. For the first time, Zeppelins carried the war in grand style far behind the front, with no escape for the civilian population. According to Olaf Grochler this meant: "... a break with the image of war ... previously formed by millions of people. ... The sharp division between front and deep hinterland had suddenly become questionable, if not invalid. Large elements of the population came to realize that they were targets for attack in a war, just like the soldiers at the front. The morale and steadfastness of the population in wartime thus took on a significance that the ruling imperialistic forces failed to recognize on the eve of the war and only grasped to a limited extent even when the war was over."[50] Graf Zeppelin's thoughts on using his airships as weapons simply ignored the suffering that must befall the civilian population as a result, and for the military it was no subject at all –

LZ 13 engine nacelle with 170-hp (125 kW) Maybach airship engine.

on the contrary, they "busied themselves with the ambitious plan of using Zeppelins to bomb New York in 1919."[51]

Zeppelins as Weapons

For years Graf Zeppelin fought to have the military administration purchase airships. When it finally happened, the Zeppelin Luftschiffbau experienced a tremendous boom. In this regard the Research Officer for Military History noted: "Recognizing the ... expected intensification of warfare, in 1899 the first Hague Peace Conference decided to ban the dropping of explosives from balloons – 'and similar new means.' After the expiration of this international agreement in 1904, however, the idea of 'using the balloon as a weapon' was again suggested, as *Generalleutnant* von Moltke stressed to the Inspectorate of Transportation Units in January 1906."[52] Zeppelin thus had an important advocate, and so after the outbreak of war a tremendous production machine began running up at Luftschiffbau Zeppelin. Zeppelins were produced at increasingly short intervals. The

Defensive position with machine-gun in the tail of a wartime airship.

Navy airships L 41 (LZ 79), L 44 (LZ 93) and L 46 (LZ 94) land in Ahlhorn after an operational flight on 21-22 August 1917.

demands of the military, for peak performance at the lowest cost, spurred chief designer Ludwig Dürr and his team to astonishing accomplishments. Between 1909 and August 1914, a total of thirteen military airships were delivered, in the following roughly fifty months until November 1918 another 88! To achieve great ranges and carry as many bombs as possible, the airships had to become larger. Between 1913 and 1917 the length increased from 158 meters (LZ 18) to 226.5 meters (LZ 104). The diameter increased from 16.6 meters to 23.93 meters, and the lifting gas volume rose from 27,000m³ to 68,500m³. Whereas LZ 18 had a range of 2100 km, a radius of action of 16,000km, for which not even the last passenger airships were designed, was demanded for LZ 104, which was supposed to undertake missions to Africa. LZ 18 was powered by four Maybach engines producing 720 HP (529 kW), which gave the airship a maximum speed of 75.6 kph, while the five Maybach engines in LZ 104 produced a total of

Command gondola of naval airship L 54 (LZ 99).

1,200 HP (882 kW), giving the ship a top speed of 103 kph. The somewhat smaller airships LZ 112, LZ 113 and LZ 114 built for the navy were even equipped with seven Maybach engines with a combined 1,820 HP (1338 kW), which accelerated the ships to 131.4 kph. The highest possible airspeed was demanded in order to be able to escape enemy aircraft. Improvements in the airships' performance were outpaced by the developments of the enemy's air defenses, however, which soon dampened the euphoric mood after several apparent military successes by the Zeppelins at the beginning of the war. Losses rose so sharply that even before the end of the war it was decided to halt the use of Zeppelin airships.[53]

Civilian Victims

In France, but especially in England, attacks by airships claimed many victims, although Kaiser Wilhelm II initially categorically refused to conduct air raids against England because of his ties to the English royal family. He ultimately gave in to pressure from the generals and the admiralty on the condition that certain areas, which obviously included Buckingham Palace in London, must never be hit, even by chance. Like other Zeppelin pilots, airship commander Ernst Lehmann had little understanding for this: "Furthermore, we found it increasingly difficult to consider non-military reservations of a purely human or even dynastic nature as the enemy made our military missions increasingly difficult."[54] In any case, with the lumbering Zeppelins it was impossible to adhere to the original demand, to bomb only militarily important and strategic targets. An example: thoroughly amused, airship captain von Buttlar related that, during a night raid, he and his bomb aimer von Schiller had "no idea" which city they had bombed and in the process had "burned their ship's number in the English soil"; this was first learned from an English newspaper.[55] In the course of fifty-one attacks by airships against English cities between January 1915 and June 1918, 498 civilians, including 110 children, were killed and 1,236 injured; fifty-eight soldiers were also killed in the attacks and 121 were wounded.[56] These figures are relatively low compared to the casualties caused by bombing in the

Navy airship L 59 (LZ 104) before its flight to Bulgaria, from where it undertook an approximately 6800 kilometer long nonstop flight to Africa and back.

Second World War, but one must always bear in mind that the Zeppelins over London began the air terror against civilian populations in the rear areas that saw its grim culmination in the destruction of Guernica, Dresden, Hiroshima and countless other cities.

Zeppelins and War Literature

Anyone who undertakes an excursion into the Zeppelin war literature, one of the most extensive chapters of the entire complex, will find it a bitter experience. Most of it is chauvinistic and from today's point of view barely readable. The following is a brief look at several lesser-known publications, that are out of the ordinary and are important aids in orientation. Georg Paul Neumann's history of the German air forces in the World War was written with the help of twenty-nine officers and officials of the army and navy aviation while the war's impact was still fresh.[57] Though written entirely in the style of the former loyal air force captain, the book is considered "useful because of the material used."[58] Paul Schmalenbach offers a profound description of the naval airships of the First World War,[59] their construction and equipment, a detailed account of the air war and extensive statistical material. Its critical description of the enormous stresses placed on the airship crews, ignored in other publications, is remarkable.[60] Wolfgang Meighörner-Schardt created a scientific work on the history of the Type "w" Zeppelin airships.[61] Two of this type were built: LZ 102 (L 57), which was destroyed on the ground in a storm shortly before its completion, and LZ 104 (L 59). They were the biggest Zeppelins built during the First World War. In Meighörner-Schardt's opinion they laid the foundation for the big airships that followed. From 21 to 25 November 1917, LZ 104 undertook a flight from Jamboli in Bulgaria to German East Africa to support the troops there under Lettow-Vorbeck.[62] The mission failed to achieve its objective, because a faked recall of the ship when it was abeam Khartoum, more than halfway to its objective, resulted in its return to Jamboli, but statistically at least it was a significant accomplishment. The ship was in the air for ninety-five hours and covered 6,756 kilometers. The original plan called for it to be completely disassembled after arriving at its destination and its various parts used for a variety of purposes. This was probably an unrealistic demand, however, as it would have required an organized landing in an area not attacked by the enemy. In order to carry the maximum payload, the builders were stingy with every gram of material in a way unlike any other Zeppelin. The long-range flight only became known to a broader audience after the war. It is now regarded as one of the outstanding Zeppelin accomplishments, alongside the successful crossing of the Atlantic by LZ 126

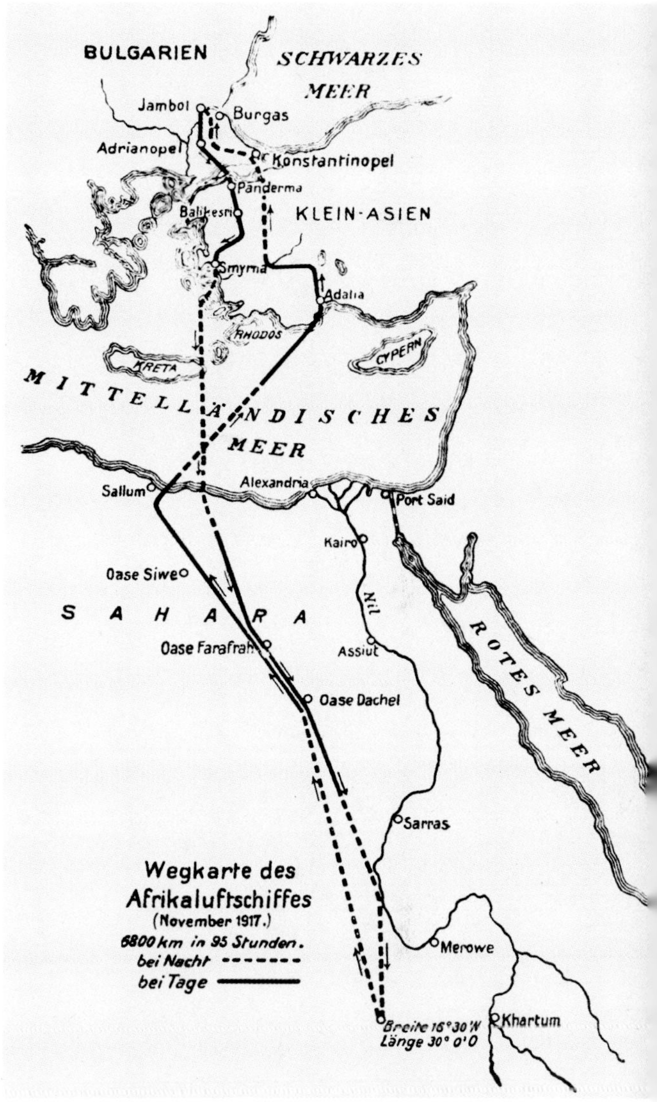

Route map of L 59's Africa flight from 21 to 25 November 1917.

The crew of L 59 for the Africa flight under Kapitänleutnant Bockholt (in center window).

in 1924. The "Africa ship" raided Italy twenty-three times, covering about 24,000 kilometers in the process. LZ 104 crashed near Otranto on 7 April 1918. There were no survivors.

New Beginning after the War

Fifteen military airships remained when the war ended. Seven of these were destroyed by their own crews on 23 June 1919 to avoid having to hand them over to the victorious powers, two days after the crews of the German High Seas Fleet scuttled their ships near the Orkney Islands. LZ 90 (LZ 120) and LZ 106 (L 61) went to Italy in 1920, LZ 109 (L 64) and LZ 113 (L 71) to England. That same year, LZ 106 had to be scrapped after a hard landing. In England the ships were not placed in service, instead they were scrapped. In July 1920 France received LZ 114, built as L 72 for the German Navy in 1918 but not taken on strength. As the *Dixmude*, the ship made a series of long-range flights over the Mediterranean, including one of 118 hours duration. On 18 December 1923 it failed to return to its base in Cuers-Pierrefeu near Toulon for reasons unknown. A few parts of the ship and the body of the commander were found, the remaining fifty-one crewmen were never found. Army airship LZ 83 (LZ 113) was delivered to France in October 1920 but was not used there. In 1920 LZ 62 (L 30) was disassembled and delivered to Belgium. One airship was also consigned to Japan. LZ 75 (L

Army airship LZ 93 (serial number LZ 63) in Dusseldorf in February 1916.

Navy airship L 70 (LZ 112), the last frontline airship, in Friedrichshafen on 1 July 1918.

37) was also disassembled and was supposed to be reassembled in a hangar in Kasumigaura near Tokyo, the structure having been moved there from Jüterbog. Japan only took delivery of several major components, however. After this there were no military airships left in Germany.

LZ 120 and LZ 121 – New Hopes

After the German Empire's surrender on 11 November 1918, Luftschiffbau Zeppelin waited anxiously for the final terms of the Treaty of Versailles. The group's general manager, Alfred Colsman, the technical director, Dr. Ludwig Dürr, the director of DELAG, Dr. Hugo Eckener, who had returned to Friedrichshafen from his position as airship trainer, as well as many of the staff and former commanders of the military airships hoped that they would soon be able to resume civil operations. The Zeppelin literature has paid little attention to the period between the end of the war and LZ 126's flight to America in 1924, which prompted Peter Kleinheins to remark: "These years, filled with naïve hopes for the future, filled with planning and entrepreneurial activity in the threatening shadow of the Treaty of Versailles and its implementing regulations, witnessed fascinating events in airship travel."[63]

Without further ado they built LZ 120 *Bodensee*, a small airship with a lifting gas capacity of just 20,000m^3, a length of 121 meters and a diameter of nineteen meters. It made its maiden flight on 20 August 1919 and, after five test flights, completed 103 flights, thirty-eight of them scheduled passenger flights between

Friedrichshafen and Berlin, before operations were shut down on 5 December. A flight from Berlin to Stockholm was supposed to be the precursor of a scheduled service to the Swedish capital, which did not materialize however. The airship flew 51,258 km and carried 4,050 persons, including 2,253 paying passengers. The ship, which was given a streamlined shape based on the calculations of Paul Jaray,[64] had three gondolas with four Maybach engines, two of which powered the aft propeller. The engines had a combined power output of 780 HP (573 kW). After the ship had been lengthened by ten meters, in July 1920 it was delivered to Italy, where, as the *Esperia*, it continued flying until 1928. Kleinheins formulated a heretofore

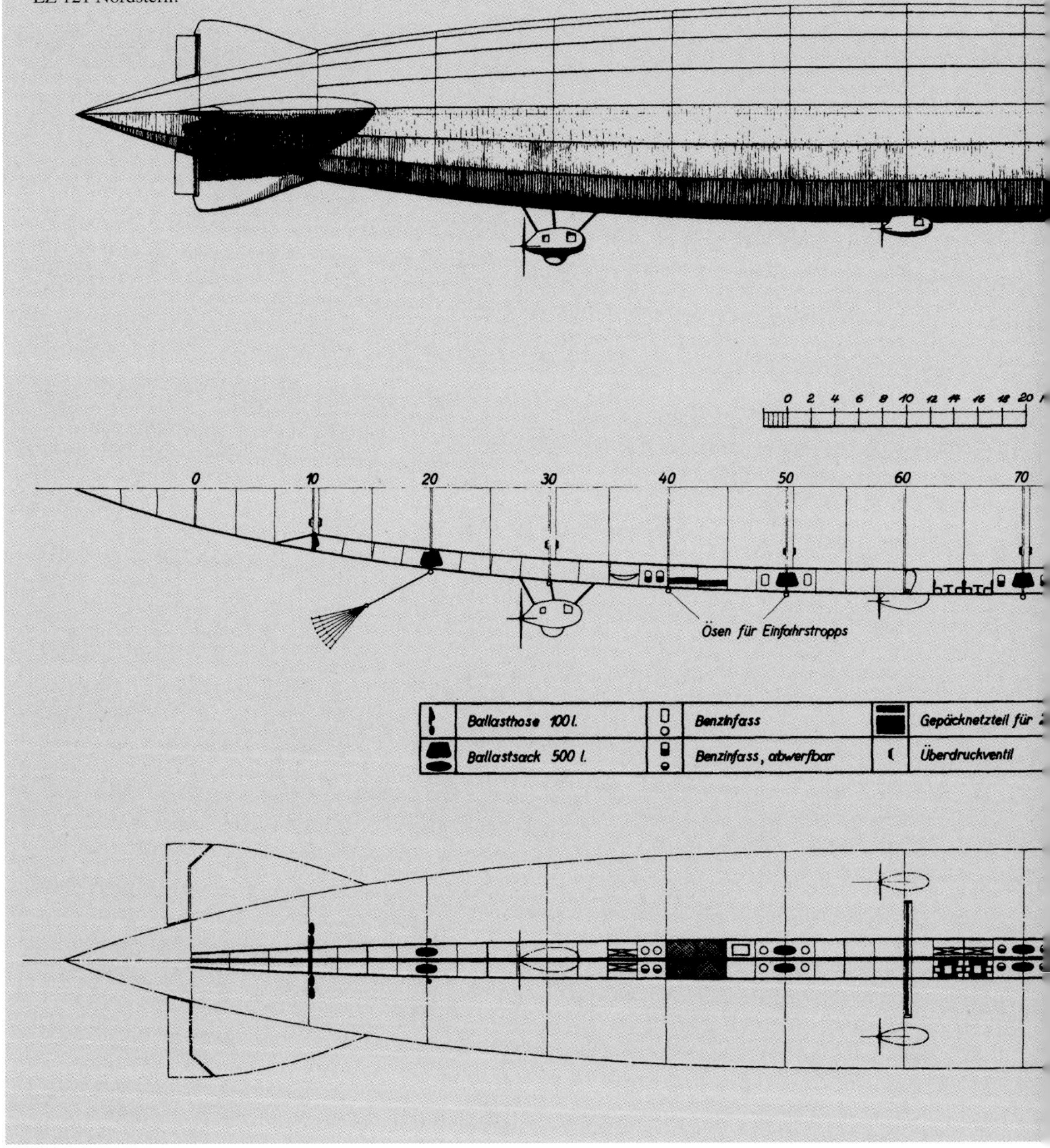

LZ 121 Nordstern.

unique list of "singular features," the most important of which are reproduced here:[65]

> first new passenger airship by LZ after ninety-six military airships;
> first scheduled service over three months;
> more ascents per day than any

Passengers on board LZ 120 Bodensee.

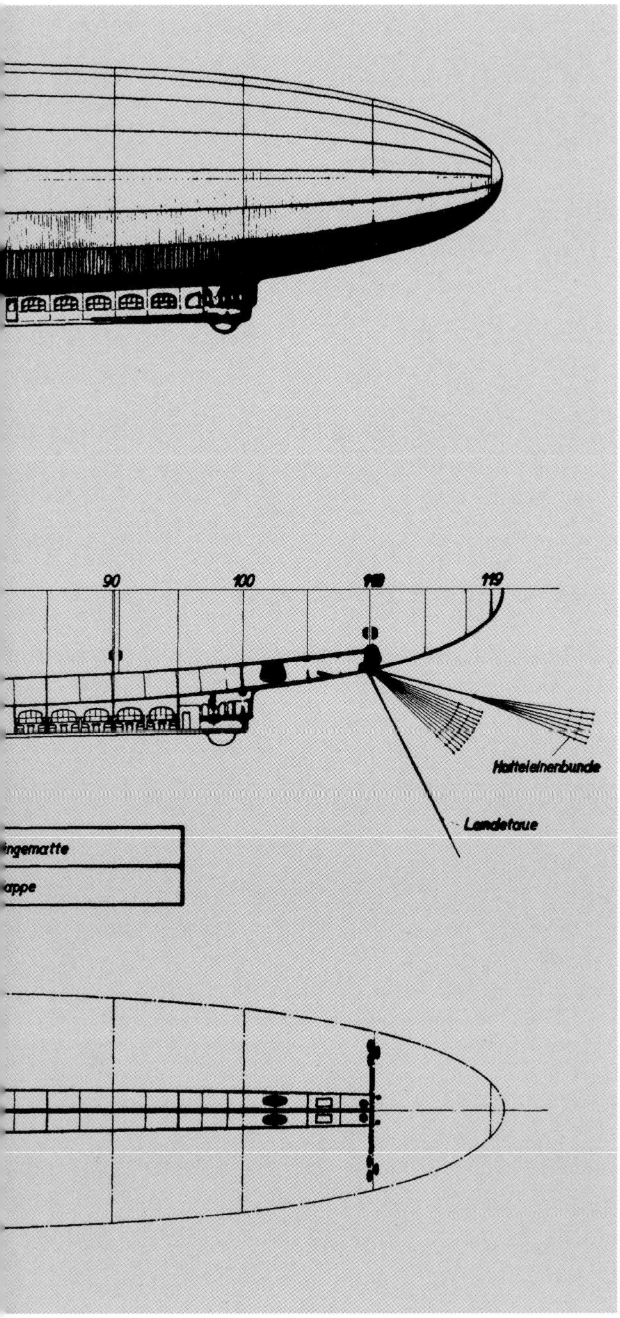

> previous commercial airship;
> longest service life of any airship (nine years);
> fastest airship in the world (130 kph);
> first Zeppelin airship with optimal streamlined shape;
> first rigid airship with dedicated crew and passenger areas beneath the fuselage;
> first experiments with active radio homing and wireless radio.

In Italy the airship was sometimes commanded by Umberto Nobile.[66]

LZ 121 *Nordstern* was built for the planned passenger service to Stockholm, but at the end of 1919, immediately after its completion, it was grounded by order of the victorious powers. Consequently the ship appears in none of DELAG's flight statistics. LZ 121 had the same dimensions and almost the same technical data as LZ 120 after the modifications. In June 1920, LZ 121 was delivered to France, where it was named *Méditerranée*. The ship was used for test and practice flights until it was scrapped in 1927.

LZ 120 Bodensee waits for passengers in its hangar.

Nord

LZ 120 Bodensee in flight.

LZ 120 Bodensee's passenger cabin.

LZ 126, the America Airship

After the surrender to the victorious powers of, not just the remaining military airships but also the two new ships LZ 120 and LZ 121, morale among the Friedrichshafen airship makers reached its nadir. There was obviously no way around the "law on the peace agreement between Germany and the allies and associated powers" of 16 July 1919, whose Article 198, Paragraph 4 succinctly declared: "No steerable airships may be kept." Plans for a transoceanic airship with a capacity of 100,000m^3 on behalf of an American steamship company were not approved, and disappeared into the desk drawer as the LZ 124 "Hensley Project," named after its initiator. The group and the jobs it provided could only be saved if they received a contract for a large airship from the government of one of the big victorious powers, and that could only be the United States. France categorically rejected any collaboration with Germany and England was building its own Zeppelin-type airships. Harry Vissering, a Chicago manufacturer, was a key figure in the development of German-American cooperation in the airship sector. A friend of American President Harding,[67]

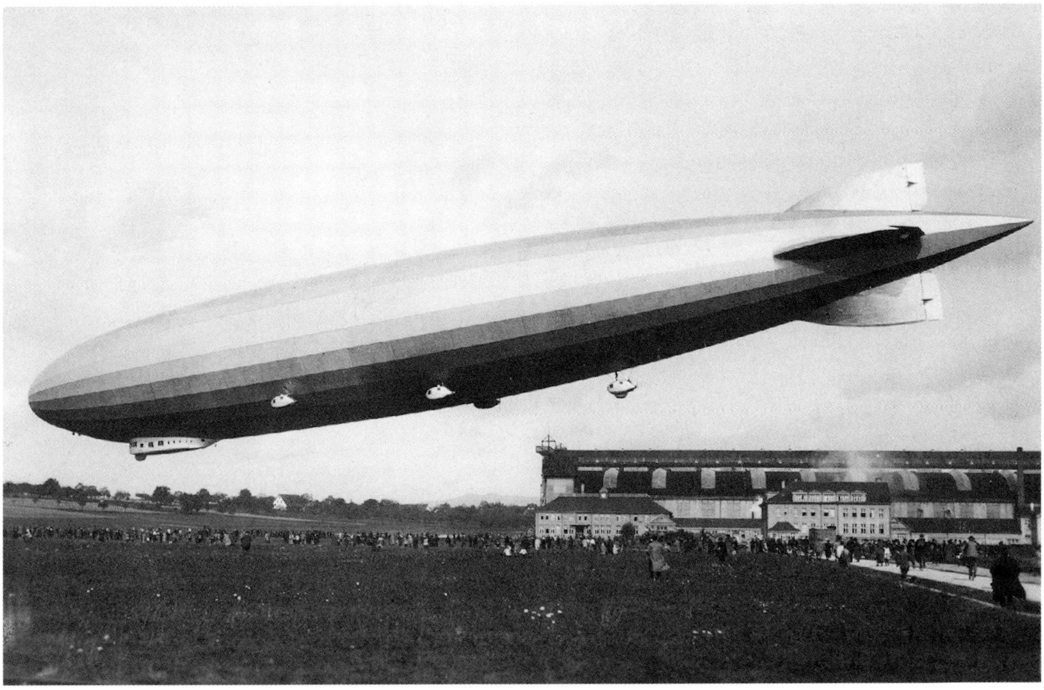

LZ 126 takes off from Friedrichshafen on a test flight.

he wisely promoted the idea in Washington that they would be out of the airship business unless they cooperated with the German airship builders. Vissering was also able to interest Paul W. Litchfield, president of the Goodyear Tire and Rubber Company, in the idea and mediate between him and Dr. Eckener, which soon resulted in close cooperation between the two concerns. And ultimately there were many more advocates. It was primarily due to Commander Charles E. Rosendahl and Vice-Admiral William A. Moffet of the navy that the government of the United States issued the contract in the sum of about three-million Marks for the building of an airship as part of the reparations owed by Germany as per the Treaty of Versailles. The project initially threatened to fail because the only method of delivering the ship was by air. There was neither approval from the German government nor any insurance company prepared to assume the insurance risk. Eckener went all out. He used all the assets of the airship group as security and then also received permission. A risk factor was completely disregarded. The United States reserved the right to decline to accept the airship after its arrival in the USA if all the conditions of the contract were not met. The technical data and required performance of the airship had been defined in the contract[68] between Luftschiffbau Zeppelin of Friedrichshafen and the Department of the Navy. The ship was to be 200 meters long, have a maximum diameter of twenty-eight meters with an overall height of thirty-two meters and a gas volume of 70,000m^3, which gave a buoyant force of 81,850kg at a barometric pressure of 760mm. Required payload was 40,000kg. The engines were supposed to produce between 2,000 and 2,500 HP (1470 - 1654 kW) and give the airship a speed of at least 112 kph. Another requirement was a strengthened nose section and special equipment for docking at anchoring masts.

During construction, the U.S. Navy maintained its own office at Luftschiffbau Zeppelin to oversee the work. The airship was given the construction number LZ 126. The length specified in the contract was strictly adhered to. The completed ship's maximum diameter was 27.64 meters. As with LZ 120 and LZ 121, the shape of the ship was designed

Meat is placed aboard LZ 126 prior to the Atlantic crossing.

Depending on the load of provisions and objects and the boarding or leaving of persons, sandbags had to be removed from or hung on the airship.

by aerodynamicist Jaray, who determined the most aerodynamic shape mathematically and practically in the wind tunnel. The streamlined shape, used from the beginning by Johann Schütte in the Schütte-Lanz airships, was adopted by Luftschiffbau Zeppelin very late – mainly for production-technical reasons – and hesitantly. Peter Kleinheins corrected the view widely-held in Zeppelin literature that Johann Schütte was the sole inventor of the streamlined shape, quoting from a memorandum by Paul Jaray from the year 1926, which is part of Jaray's bequest to the Swiss Technical University in Zurich: "As is well known, Schütte reserved to himself the claim of having built airships based on 'scientific principles', and declared that LZ 'copied' his successful work. In reality all of the LZ innovations in question came from my office, and during the war I relied exclusively on myself and my research, while I had no idea of what was happening in other companies, including Schütte-Lanz."[69] In any case the fuselage dimensions resulted in the required capacity of 70,000m³. Five twelve-cylinder Maybach engines produced a combined 2,000 HP (1 470 kW). Estimated maximum speed was 124.2 kph. The ship made its maiden flight on 27 August 1924 and it was determined that the requested performance figures had been met.

The tensely-awaited Atlantic crossing took place from the 12th to 16th of October. On board were twenty-seven crewmen plus three guests from the U.S. Navy and one from the U.S. Army. The airship was commanded by Hugo Eckener. The eighty-five-hour flight was made without serious incident. The importance of this flight to diplomatic and economic relations between the two countries cannot be overestimated. When the ship arrived over New York it was greeted by a cacophony of fire alarms from the city and ship's horns in the harbor. Thousands of people had gathered at the landing site in Lakehurst, New Jersey. During a reception for the airship's officers at the White House in Washington, President Coolidge[70] characterized the airship as a messenger of peace with which Germany would again find acceptance in the community of nations after the years of war. From then on there was no more talk of a ban on the construction of airships. LZ 126, now called ZR 3 *Los Angeles*, had not only brought immeasurable economic benefits to Luftschiffbau Zeppelin, but had also filled an unexpected political function which was to have lasting effects on relations between Germany and the USA. Together with Ernst Lehmann and Hans von Schiller, who had participated in the flight as duty officer and navigation officer respectively, Eckener travelled through the States to establish contacts for the world airship service planned by Luftschiffbau Zeppelin. Lehmann spent some time at the Goodyear Tire and Rubber Company in Akron, Ohio to deepen the relationship that had existed since the signing of the agreement for the formation of the Goodyear Zeppelin

After successfully crossing the Atlantic, LZ 126 was handed over to the U.S. Navy; the ship, seen here over Washington, was subsequently called ZR 3 Los Angeles.

Corporation on 19 September 1923. A part of the crew also remained in the USA for a time to train the American crew of the *Los Angeles*.

LZ 127 *Graf Zeppelin*

Although LZ 126's success also made an impression in Germany, the Reich government was still skeptical and initially unprepared to provide funds for the construction of another large airship. By then it was felt that the future of aviation lay in aircraft.

The Zeppelin-Eckener Fund Makes it Possible

Dr. Eckener therefore took another path. He built on the emotional enthusiasm of the German people and for months he and crewmen from LZ 126 hit the speaking circuit, showed slides of the trip to America and raising about 2.5-million Marks in a fund-raising effort called the Zeppelin-Eckener Fund. This was equivalent to about a third of the cost of the planned new airship. LZ 127 was 236.6 meters long and its fuselage had a maximum diameter of 30.5 meters; the dimensions were determined by the size of existing hangars. Seventeen cells contained 105,000m^3 of hydrogen gas. Five Maybach engines with a combined output of 2,650 HP (1,948 kW) propelled the ship to a maximum of 110.2 kph. Radius of action was supposed to be 12,000 km. As with LZ 126, the command gondola and passenger gondola for twenty passengers were designed as a single

A ground handling crew for ZR 3 Los Angeles; in the background there is a huge gathering of news reporters and film crews.

unit beneath the front of the airship. LZ 127 was dubbed the *Graf Zeppelin* and made its first test flight on 18 September 1928. Hans von Schiller, who captained the ship for many years, described it from his point of view: "The earlier DELAG ships had only undertaken short flights. With the *Graf Zeppelin* we intended to remain airborne for up to five days. There were therefore day and night quarters for the passengers and crew plus toilets and washrooms. An electric kitchen provided those on board with normal hot meals. While the luxury on board the Zeppelin could not compare with the service on a steamship, the passenger cabin had windows, some of which could be opened, and a lovely salon was used to take meals and spend time comfortably. Just one thing was missing on the airship: seasickness. We had actually built the *Graf Zeppelin* only as an experimental ship for long-range flights, for before introducing a regular long-range service with a specially-designed Zeppelin, we planned to conduct experimental flights in all climates and zones of the earth, over the oceans and continents in every part of the world."[71]

LZ 127's flight characteristics also met all expectations. In October 1928 they made one last test flight that lasted thirty-four hours and took the ship as far as the North Sea, and on 11 October it took off with a full load of passengers on its first flight to America. Because of the long duration of the flight, a three watch system similar to that on ships at sea had to be used, so that, apart from the captain, officers alternated between four hours watch and eight hours rest. Including several aspiring airship crewmen, which were present on almost every flight, the usual crew complement was forty-six.

The airship's arrival in the USA was even more triumphant than LZ 126's had been four years earlier. It remained there for four weeks because of a defect in the tail section that had developed during the flight, but the time was used to the full to make contacts. Among others, Eckener met automobile and engine makers Henry Ford, Walter Chrysler and others to discuss matters concerning the world airship

The assembly of the individual beam parts of the structure, which were basically riveted together, required good power of imagination (above).

The nose section of LZ 127; this had to be a particularly robust structure, as the ship was anchored on it.

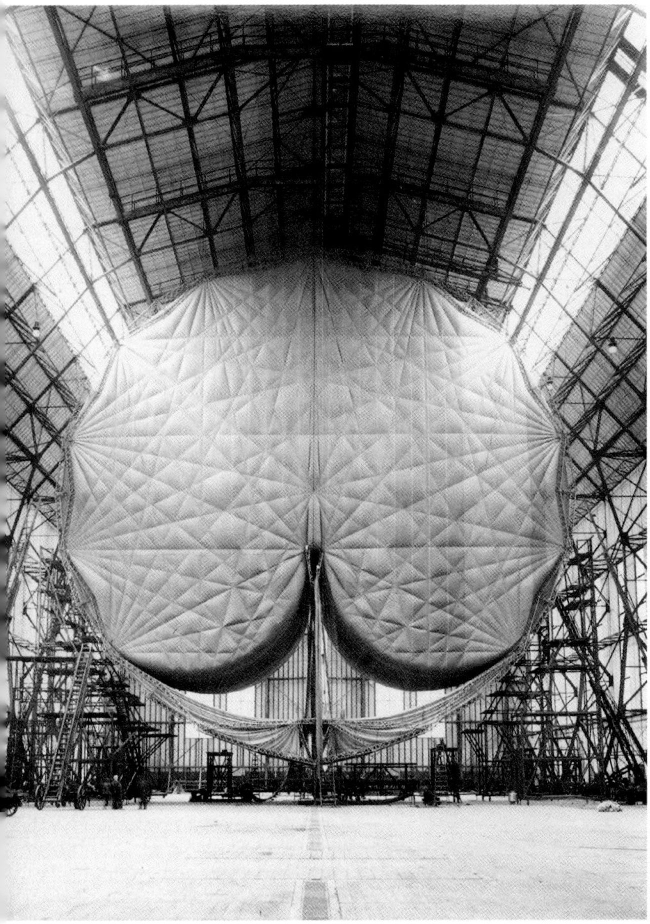

One of LZ 127's gas cells is filled during a test; the complex ring tensioning leaves its impression on the cell. LZ 127's fuselage framework – still without nose section – from the front (facing page).

service, including the infrastructure issue, in which these persons were of course interested. LZ 127 took off on the return flight on 29 October with twenty-four passengers. The next day they were joined by the first stowaway in aviation, a nineteen-year-old American who had come aboard with a mailbag. He was forced to help out in the kitchen and caused quite a sensation when the ship arrived in Friedrichshafen.

The 1929 Round-the World Flight

There followed a whole series of long flights designed to increase operating experience before the now famous round-the-world flight. The American publisher W.C. Hurst acquired exclusive world rights, excluding Europe, to coverage of the flight, which covered most of the costs. The rest of the financing came from other newspapers and not least philately. Specially-stamped letters and postage stamps carried on the round-the-world trip are still popular among collectors of air mail. Apart from journalists, because of the high cost, few paying passengers made the flight. In return for his large investment, Hearst demanded that the round-the-world flight should begin and end in Lakehurst or at the Statue of Liberty in New York. And so, on 1 August 1929, LZ 129 first flew to Lakehurst before taking off again on 8 August for Friedrichshafen, where on the 10th of August, Eckener's 61st birthday, it landed after a record-setting time of fifty-five hours and nineteen minutes. Four more days were needed to prepare the ship for its long voyage. The airship actually began the round-the-world flight on 15 August with a total of sixty people on board, Hans von Schiller wrote: "We flew over Königsberg and Berlin ... into Russia. On the second day we crossed the Urals, we had left Europe. The forests were endless; we often flew over huge forest fires with enormous clouds of smoke that obscured everything. Those on board were a colorful group, mainly journalists. Journalism predominated. Our radio operators sat sweating in the radio compartment from morning till night, dispatching endlessly long news telegrams in every possible language, even Japanese. The performance of the radio personnel was terrific, for in addition to sending press telegrams they also had to receive frequent weather reports. Our radio room never lost its sense of humor, however, and it held out and made a significant contribution to the success of the flight."[72]

Despite inadequate maps, the airship found its way across the vastness of Siberia and after a ninety-hour flight landed in Tokyo. Mankind had never seen anything like it: after a single flight they had landed in a completely different cultural area.

The ship took off from Tokyo on the second leg of the flight. In sixty-eight hours it crossed the Pacific Ocean. As planned, the airship made landfall at the Golden Gate near San Francisco. It then landed at an anchor mast in Los Angeles. Unexpected difficulties were

Twin cabin on board LZ 127 (above) and at night (below).

The common room in LZ 127 set up for taking meals (above left) and as a lounge (below left). Despite its weight, Luftschiffbau Zeppelin GmbH had expensive porcelain made by the manufacturer Heirich of Selb and its own silverware.

encountered during the takeoff for Lakehurst, the penultimate leg of the trip. Hans von Schiller: "It was much warmer than expected, consequently our calculations as to the amount of hydrogen gas needed to top up the cells were off. Dr. Eckener decided on the spot to leave one of the three-crew watches on the ground. They would later follow by aircraft to Lakehurst. All of the excess water and provisions were unloaded. Spare parts that didn't appear to be absolutely necessary had to stay behind. Finally it seemed to be working! The airship rose, but at a height of about forty meters there was an inversion, a layer of warmer air, which reduced the airship's lift. It stopped climbing Full ahead was selected on all engines. Slowly, slowly, it began to climb. Then, suddenly, a huge high-tension line ahead. The hazard lights on the mast tips glowed red. Even then Dr. Eckener kept his cool. To his son, who had watch on the elevator controls, he merely said quite calmly: just a little higher. We passed over the line by at most five meters."[73]

After twenty-one days, LZ 127 Graf Zeppelin again circled the Statue of Liberty. It had successfully circumnavigated the northern hemisphere. Without Eckener, who remained in the USA for negotiations, two days later Captain Ernst Lehmann took off for Friedrichshafen, where the ship arrived safely after travelling 36,000 kilometers.

Loading provisions.

LZ 127 Graf Zeppelin during landing.

A crowd gathered around the airship in Berlin.

LZ 127 Graf Zeppelin in flight.

LZ 127 Graf Zeppelin over Berlin.

During its world flight of 1929, LZ 127 Graf Zeppelin casts its shadow over huge woodpiles in Arkhangelsk (above); the airship over Tokyo (below).

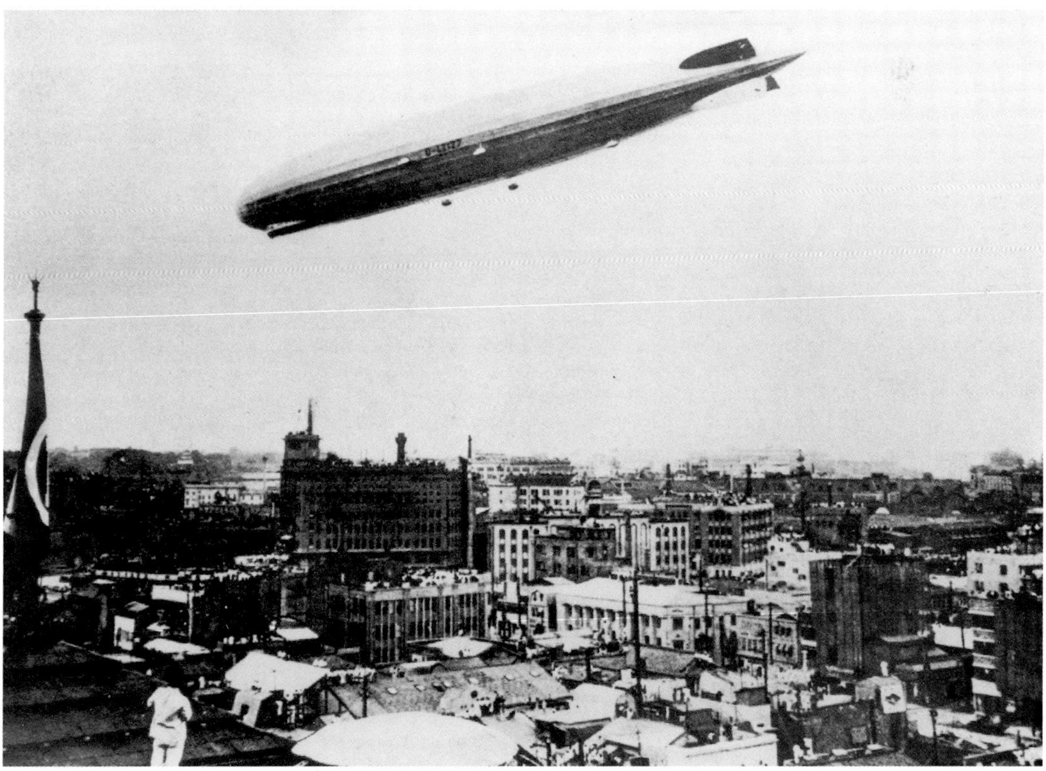

Gas cylinders for the Graf Zeppelin stockpiled in Kasumigaura near Tokyo, Japan.

During its round-the-world flight, the Graf Zeppelin joins a Goodyear blimp at the anchor mast in Los Angeles.

The airship over Manhattan.

Photographed from an aircraft, LZ 127 Graf Zeppelin over El Paso on the border between the USA and Mexico in 1929 (above).

LZ 127 Graf Zeppelin back in Friedrichshafen after the first circumnavigation of the northern hemisphere (below).

LZ 127 Graf Zeppelin in the giant hangar at Lakehurst in New Jersey.

After its round-the-world flight, which had begun in Friedrichshafen on 15 August 1929, the airship received an enthusiastic welcome on its return to Friedrichshafen on 4 September.

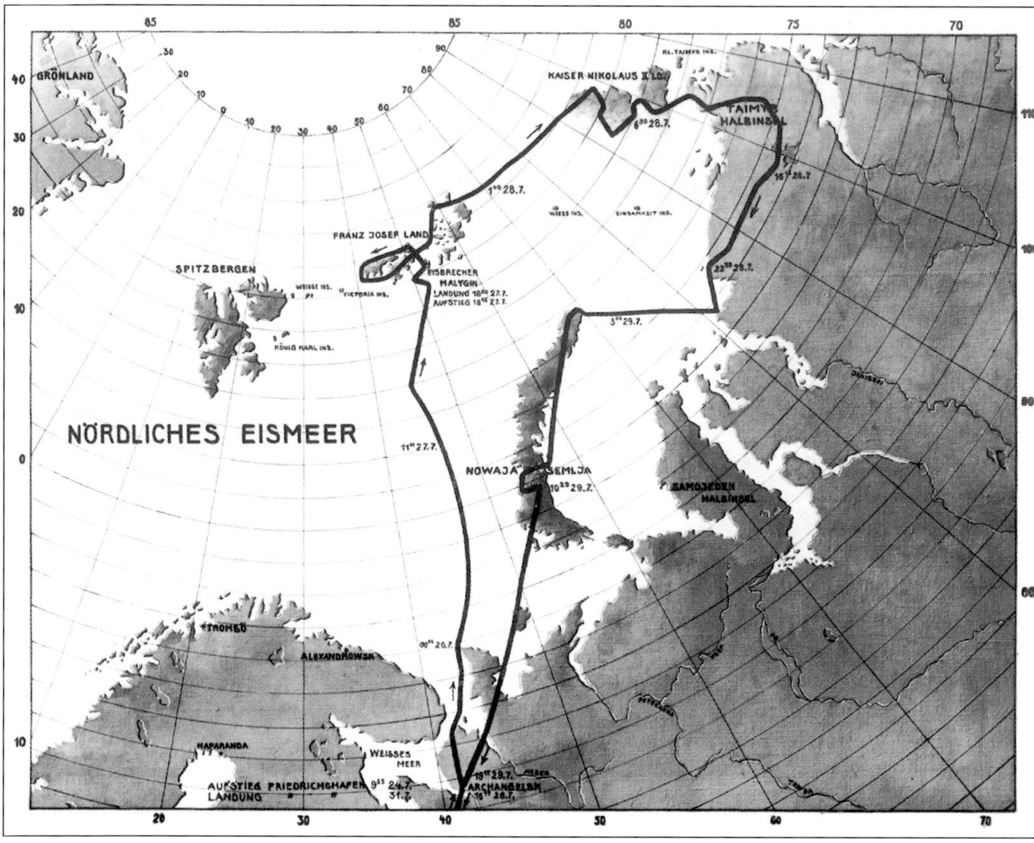

The route during the Arctic flight of 1931 passed over regions that had been little known until then.

The Arctic Flight 1931

When man achieved the ability to move about in the air, inaccessible areas of the world suddenly became of interest, for it was thought that it must be easy to explore uncharted areas from the air. The Arctic had long been one such region. Even Graf Zeppelin had shown interest in the area and in 1910 had undertaken an expedition to Spitzbergen with the Lloyd steamship *Mainz*, whose captain was Max Dietrich, who later became a navy airship commander. On this trip Professor Adolf Miethe[74] took his first color photos, which became famous around the world.

1931 was declared the "Polar Year" in order to encourage research in the Arctic on an international level. In 1929 Fridtjof Nansen[75] had sought out Eckener and asked him to use an airship for this, as it appeared to be an ideal research platform. The Zeppelin could cover long distances, fly slowly at low altitude, even remain stationary, it could land on water as well as solid ground, and it could operate for days before having to be resupplied. After Nansen's death, in 1930 Dr. Hugo Eckener had become president of Aeroarctic, an international company for Arctic research with air vehicles. The company's general secretary was the former army airship commander Walter Bruns. As Eckener had shown an interest in Nansen's wish, LZ 127 was repurposed as a research ship. It was planned, for example, to carry out cartographic tasks, for which the airship was particularly well suited, because cameras had to be positioned far apart to take stereo photographs. Twin compasses were installed to measure deviation and the earth's magnetic field. Atmospheric measurements would be made using a radiosonde carried aloft by a balloon. Another research topic was the formation of rock in areas with extreme climates. On board the airship in addition to six German scientists were two American, three Soviet and one Swedish researcher. They were joined by a German journalist Arthur Köstler,[76] a press photographer and a film reporter. The crew of thirty, including a radio operator from the USSR, was under Eckener's command. From the standpoint of safety the expedition was prepared meticulously. Hans von Schiller: "Scientific equipment had to be installed in the catwalk and in the cabins. The participants in the expedition were divided into tent communities, each consisting of four men. For each tent there was a gas stove and dishes, reindeer skin sleeping bags and wool blankets. Each man was issued Arctic clothing and plenty of Arctic underwear plus a sewing kit. The basic food was pemmican, the proven Arctic diet. Hunting and fishing equipment was taken along to enable the party to supplement its diet with fresh meat and fish. Ten sleighs, equipped with Nirosta stainless steel skis based on Nansen's experience, were envisaged for moving camp. Two kayaks were also brought along. They were to be used for crossing waterways. All the polar equipment weighed almost fifteen tons and in the event of an involuntary stay would have kept the party in supplies for more than a year."[77]

LZ 127 took off from Friedrichshafen on 24 July 1931. After a stop in Berlin to collect the remaining items of equipment, the voyage continued over Königsberg, Riga, Reval, Helsingfors (Helsinki) to Leningrad, where the Soviet scientists came aboard. The party was then complete, with a total of forty-six persons on board. The airship proceeded via Arkhangelsk to Franz-Josephs-Land, where it arrived on 27 July. LZ 127 came down in a bay and exchanged philatelist mail with the Soviet icebreaker *Mallygin*. The attempt to deliver mail and food to a research station on Severnaya Zemlya failed because of bad weather. Other, successful, experiments included those with the balloon, which took measurements of the atmosphere up to a height of 14,000 meters and was in radio contact with the airship. A probe lowered from the airship to just above the surface of the water provided information about the air beneath the ship, making possible the creation of a complete profile of the entire then relevant atmosphere. The flight continued to Cape Chelyuskin, the northernmost point of the Eurasian continent, then back in a wide arc to the east over Novaya Zemlya. The airship returned to Leningrad via Arkhangelsk but was unable to land there because of bad weather, so Eckener decided to fly to Berlin. LZ 127 landed there on the evening of 30 July. It had covered 13,309 kilometers in 145 hours and twenty-six minutes of flying time. The scientists on the airship brought back a wealth of scientific information.

Exchange of mail between LZ 127 Graf Zeppelin and the Soviet freighter Malygin in the northern Arctic Ocean; the airship has descended onto the surface of the water.

Cartographers at work on the Graf Zeppelin during the Arctic flight.

Mail and Passenger Service

LZ 127 was refitted as a passenger ship and made three flights to South America in 1931. Because of the great interest, it had been decided to expand service to South America and reduce the number of shorter flights in Europe. A round-trip flight in 1930 served as preparation for this. LZ 127 departed Friedrichshafen and stopped in Seville, Recife de Pernambuco, Rio de Janeiro, Lakehurst and back over Seville to Friedrichshafen. An important aspect of experimental flights over the Atlantic was determining the most favorable wind conditions on the westbound and eastbound routes. The flights had to be halted during the tropical rainy period. During those weeks shorter flights were made in Europe, which the Zeppeliners disrespectfully called "circus flights."

The South America trips were not just about carrying passengers. Mail shipments also played an increasing role in financing the flights. The result was the development of a sophisticated transport system, in which various means of transportation were involved, as described by Hans von Schiller: "Whereas the 'Graf Zeppelin' had flown one-hundred-thousand kilometers in 1931, in 1932 it was two-hundred-thousand. And operations continued to expand from year to year. Operations reached their peak in 1936 with a fourteen-day schedule, during which we made sixteen trips to Rio de Janeiro. Beginning in 1934 there was also good cooperation with Deutsche Lufthansa in the carrying of mail. While the Zeppelin took off from Friedrichshafen at ten in the evening, the next morning a Heinkel Blitz, capable of more than 300 kilometers per hour, took off from Berlin and overtook us over the Canary Islands. At Gando airfield they loaded the mail onto a truck, which drove to the downwind side of the field. We flew over it at a height of about 100 meters and lowered a rope. Driving as precisely into the wind as possible, the truck followed our rope, attaching mail bags weighing up to 100kg to its snap hook. We brought the mail on board. If there was more than 100kg we had to make another pass. At Recife de Pernambuco in South America, an aircraft was waiting for us. After we landed we transferred the mailbags to it. When we couldn't land we dropped them by parachute. The aircraft flew the mail ahead to Rio de Janeiro, from where it was flown to Santiago de Chile by a Ju 52. There they had eight to ten hours before the Ju 52 took off for Buenos Aires and flew the mail back to Recife. In this way it was possible to send a letter from Berlin to Santiago and receive a reply seven days later. We also worked in other ways with Lufthansa, which had also established a direct airmail service to South America. Aircraft brought the mail to Bathurst on the African coast. There it was transferred to one of the catapult ships *Westfalen* or *Schwabenland*, one of which was stationed on the African and one on the Brazilian coast – usually near Fernando de Noronha. The mail aircraft was shot from the ship by catapult and crossed the ocean. But as the catapult ships were slow and were usually anchored at their stations, in these tropical waters a great deal of vegetation grew on the ships' hulls. Each year, therefore, they had to go to a shipyard. During this period the Zeppelin took over the mail service, operating a shuttle service between Bathurst and Recife for about four weeks."[78]

LZ 127 Graf Zeppelin has landed; the ground handling team maneuvers the airship into the hangar (above), after the confusion on the retaining webs had been resolved (right).

In March 1935 Hans von Schiller became captain of LZ 127 *Graf Zeppelin*. That year the airship flew 350,000 kilometers on the South-American route, carrying 4,000kg of mail, 572

Inside LZ 127's control room; on the left are the elevator controls, in the middle the rudder controls.

Passengers were permitted to inspect the gloomy and strange interior of the huge airship, but only in small groups with close supervision.

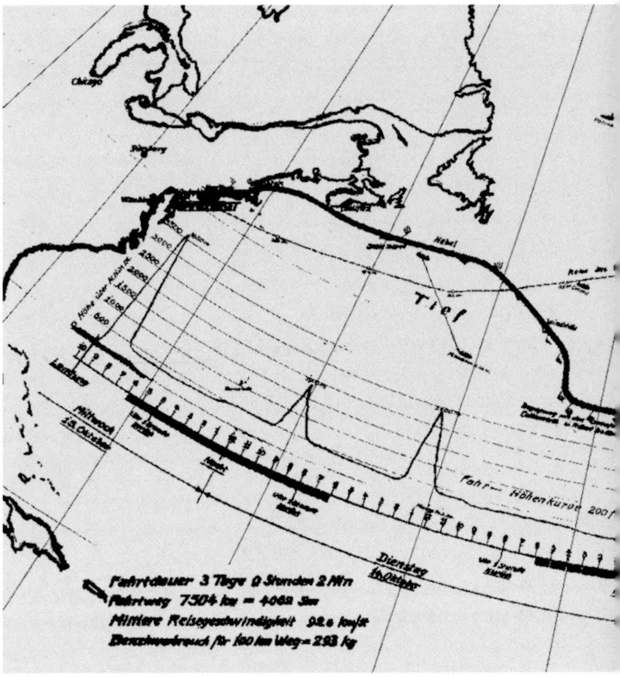

LZ 127's route of flight from Friedrichshafen to Lakehurst, USA. The route was largely determined by weather conditions; for comparison, the route taken by a passenger steamer is marked above. LZ 127 Graf Zeppelin at the mobile anchor mast in Lakehurst (below).

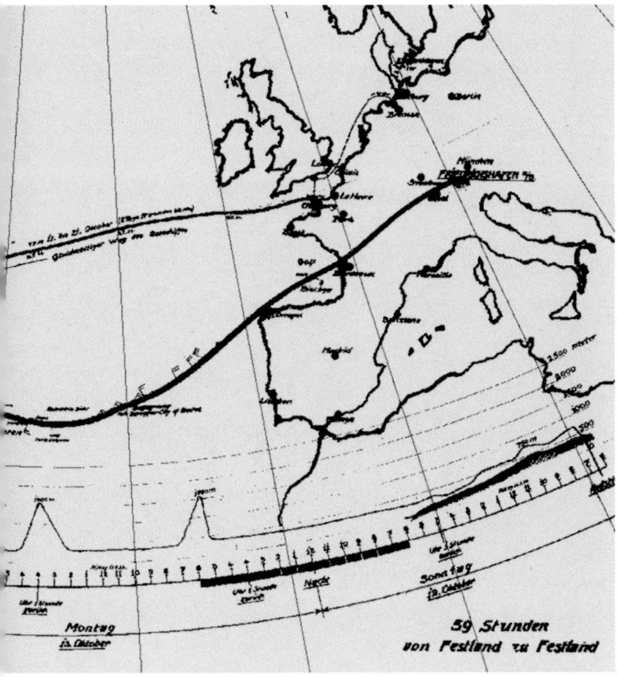

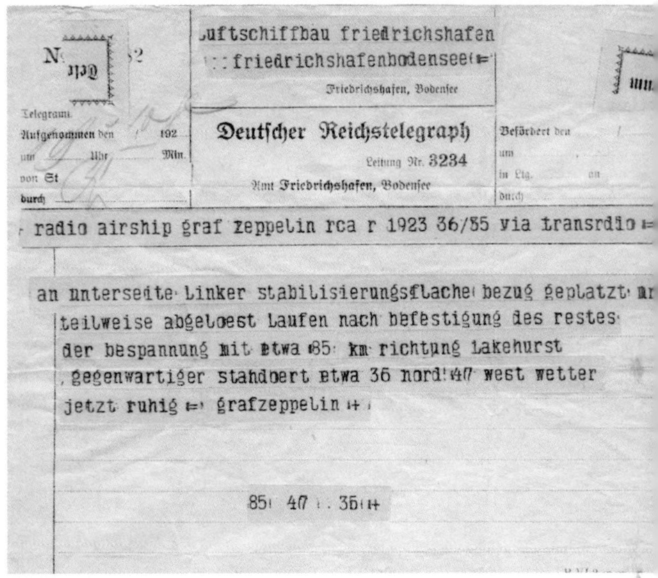

Luftschiffbau friedrichshafen
friedrichshafenbodensee
Friedrichshafen, Bodensee

Telegramm
Aufgenommen den 192
um Uhr Min.
von St
durch

Deutscher Reichstelegraph
Leitung Nr. 3234
Amt Friedrichshafen, Bodensee

Befördert den
um
in Ltg. an
durch

radio airship graf zeppelin rca r 1923 36/55 via transrdio =

an untersedte linker stabilisierungsflache bezug geplatzt und teilweise abgeloest laufen nach befestigung des restes der bespannung mit etwa 85 km richtung lakehurst gegenwartiger standoert etwa 36 nord 47 west wetter jetzt ruhig = grafzeppelin +

85 47 . 35 +

During the first flight to America, one of LZ 127's stabilizers was damaged in a storm; as the telegram above states, after repairs the ship continued on its way at reduced speed.

Carrying mail soon became a profitable business for the airship company; a special stamp was used on almost every flight.

passengers and 5,000kg of freight. Eckener even wanted to send LZ 127 to Buenos Aires on a regular basis, but that probably would have been expecting too much of the ship and the necessary logistical and technical organization. "We flew there once in 1934, but, because of the frequent *pamperos*, the general weather situation seemed to us to exceed the performance capabilities of the airship. A faster ship would be required to begin this long-range service."

LZ 127 began scheduled service to South America in August 1931; the photo shows the airship on the anchor mast in Pernambuco.

Rendezvous in the South Atlantic; LZ 127 Graf Zeppelin overflies the Italian steamer Neptunia.

LZ 127 Graf Zeppelin cruises into the bay of Rio de Janeiro.

Return to Friedrichshafen from a long-distance flight.

People were fascinated whenever an airship appeared in the sky, as here over a railway station in Berlin.

The airship encounters an aircraft; the crew in the forward starboard gondola wave.

LZ 127 Graf Zeppelin over the harbor entrance in Lindau on Lake Constance.

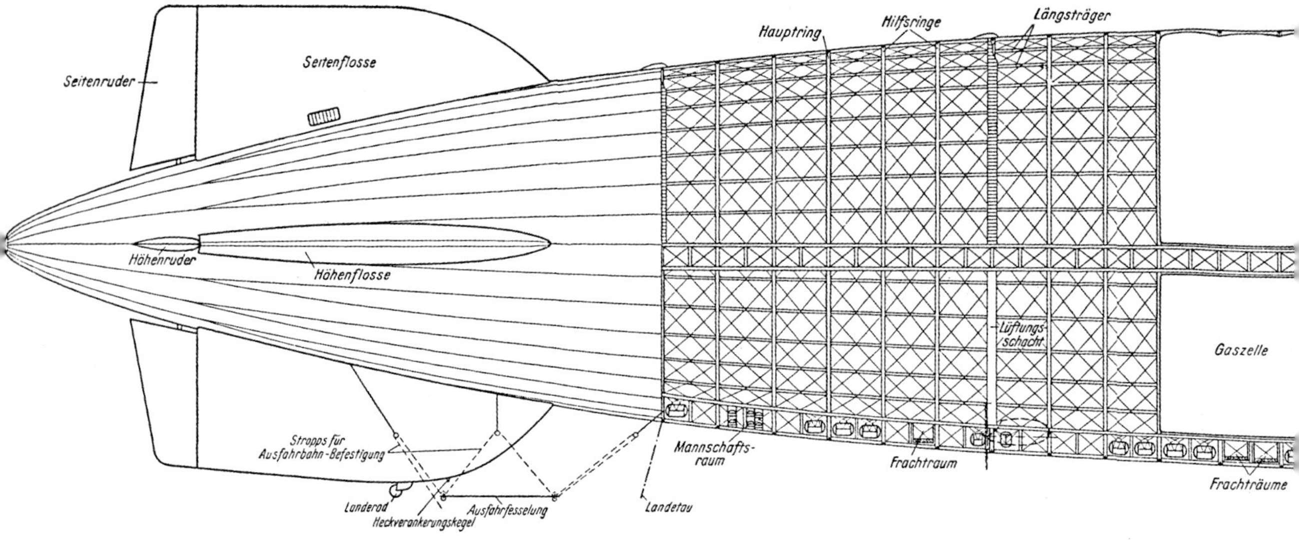

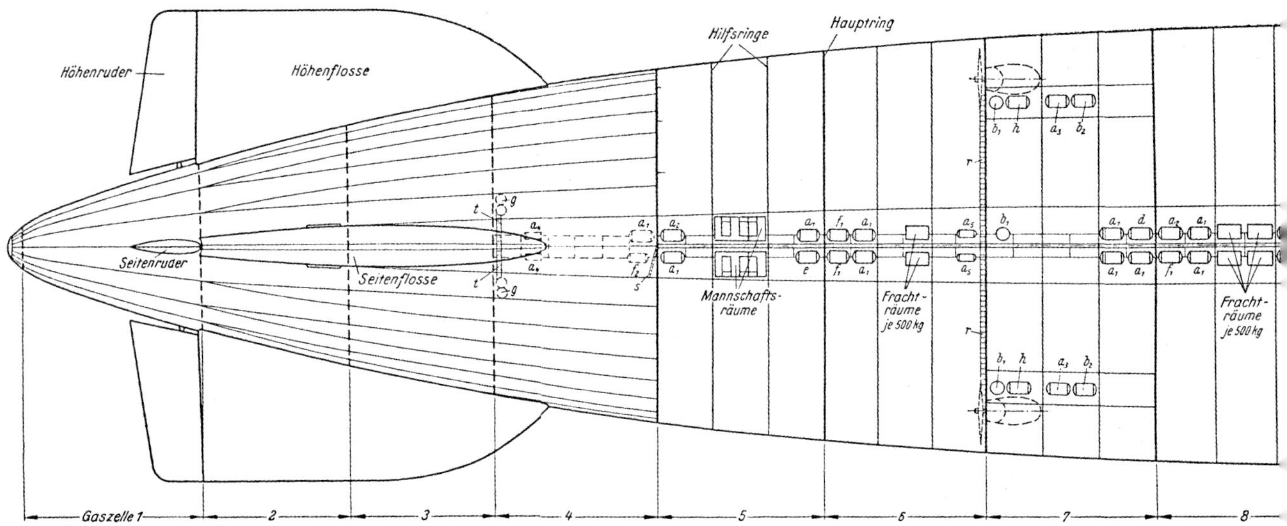

LZ 129 *Hindenburg*

The airship LZ 129 *Hindenburg* was built for longer ranges and better overall performance. It made its maiden flight on 4 March 1936. LZ 129 was a giant, the largest air vehicle ever in commercial passenger service. As always, Director Dürr was in overall charge of construction. With a maximum lifting gas capacity of 200,000m^3, the fuselage had almost twice the volume of LZ 127's, which was primarily due to its streamlined form, which, with a length-to-diameter ratio[80] of 5.9, was very near to the ideal aerodynamic shape. Overall length was 245 meters and maximum diameter 41.2 meters. The only airship with a similarly favorable length-to-diameter ratio was LZ 120, with 6.5. The figure for LZ 127 was 7.8, which was determined by the dimensions of the available construction hangar. LZ 129's shape, which at first glance looked plump, had very good aerodynamic characteristics, enabling the huge airship to reach a maximum speed of 131kph. It was powered by four Daimler diesel engines with a combined output of 4,200 HP (3087 kW). LZ 129 was the first Zeppelin expressly designed for long-range passenger service. A very significant change compared to LZ 127 was the separation of the command gondola and the passenger rooms. The latter were in the interior of the ship. Only the command gondola projected beneath the ship fuselage. It was of course aerodynamically-shaped and also offered a clear view backward. The following description of the ship is largely based on the publication by Wilhelm Ernst Dörr[81], reproduced in summarized form. The description corresponds to the condition of the ship on completion.[82]

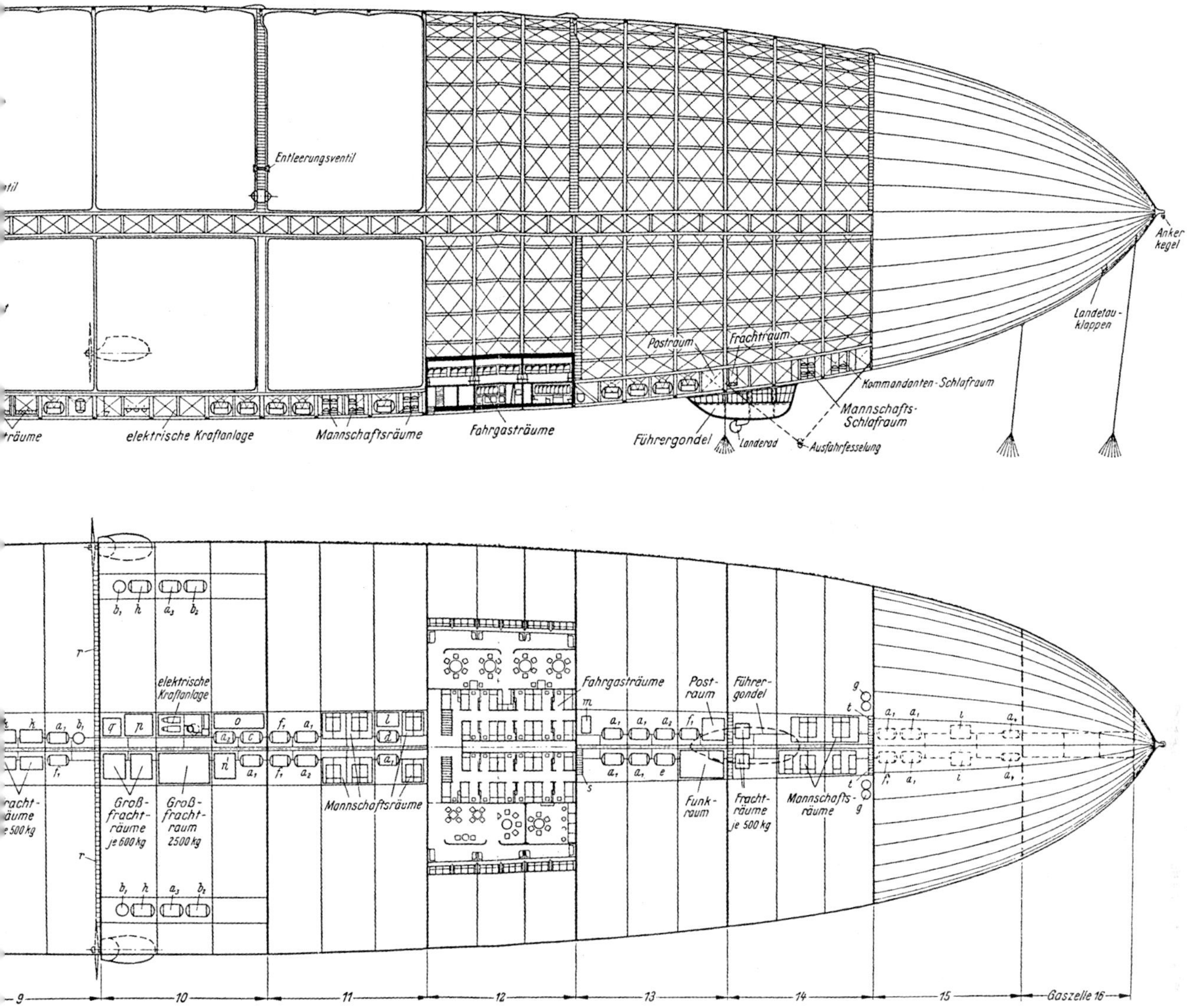

Side (above) and overhead views of LZ 129 Hindenburg (by W.E. Dörr 1936). The passenger areas are located in the forward third of the airship (black outlined area in the upper drawing). The drawing clearly illustrates the tremendous effort required by the "lighter than air" system to carry a small payload.

Bottom drawing:

a	Fuel tanks	l and m	Food storeroom
b	Lubricating oil reservoir	n	Engineer room
c	Drinking water tank	o	Ventilator
d	Fresh water tank	p	Crew washroom and toilet
e	Waste water tank	q	Workshop
f	Tank for recovered ballast water	r	Passages to the engines
g	Ballast water hoses	s	Accesses to the ladder shafts
h	Coolant water tank	t	Accesses to the ballast hoses
i	Baggage compartment		
k	Spare parts storage compartment		

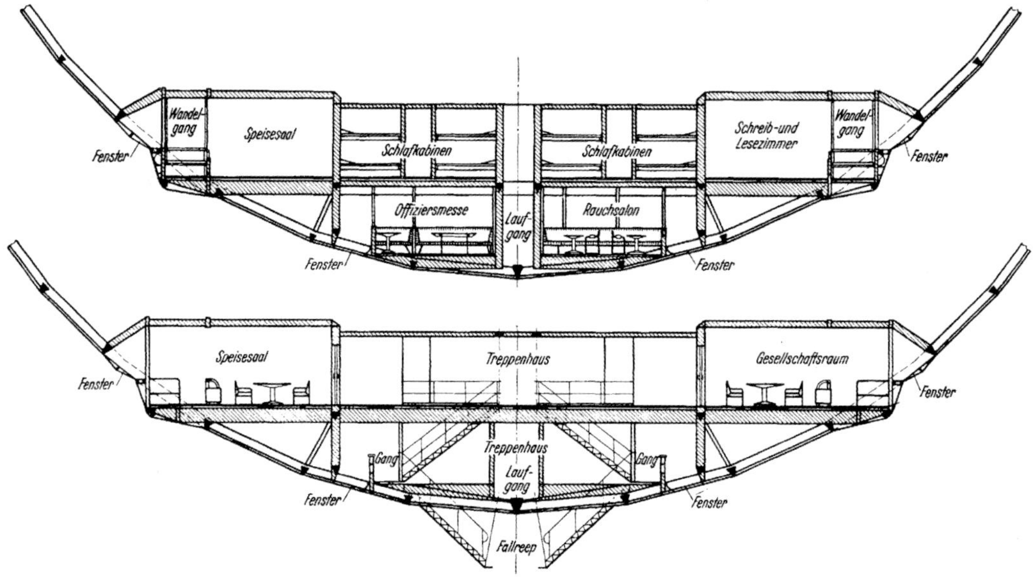

Section through the cabins and day rooms (above) and section at the level of the staircase and the day rooms (below) of LZ 129.

Cross-section through the cruciform tail.

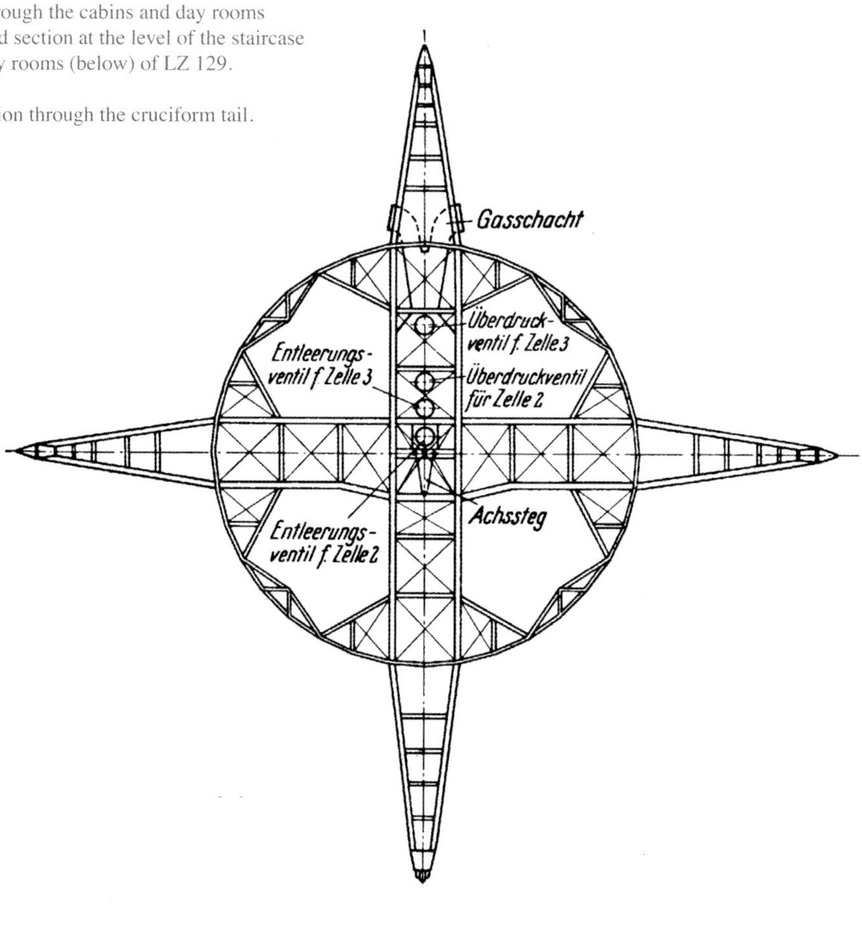

The cruciform tail under construction.

The Framework Structure

LZ 129 also used the proven triangular beams, which were proportioned according to the size of the airship. The tips of the triangles faced outwards on the girders, inwards on the ring beams. Hexagonal open section profiles with stabilizing cross sections formed the corners of the beams, which were stiffened by specially formed profiles and riveted to them. Thirty-six girders, whose number decreased towards the nose and tail, joined fifteen main rings arranged at intervals of about fifteen meters, whose inwards-facing truss bearers were guyed to the axial catwalk with wires. Between each pair of main rings there were two auxiliary rings, which were not braced against the catwalk. The braced main rings divided the interior of the fuselage into sixteen compartments for the accommodation of the gas cells. The three main rings in the tail were excluded from the bracing, but instead were stiffened by a ring cross which joined the external stabilizers. The rings were assembled horizontally on the ground. A special assembly ring was used to raise them into a vertical position for assembly of the fuselage framework.

The nose was strengthened and fitted with special equipment for anchoring the ship to the mast, which will be described in "Airship Hangars and Landings Masts" later in the book. The keel gangway extended from the nose cap ring to the leading edges of the stabilizers. In the area of the engine gondolas, connecting passages with hatches led outwards. The engine gondolas could be reached by ladders. Three vertical ladders provided access to the axial catwalk, which extended from nose to tail.

Of the aerodynamically shaped stabilizers, which had their own internal framework, the bottom one was smaller to avoid damage during takeoff and landing. A movable landing wheel was positioned at its lowest point.

The framework of Zeppelin airship LZ 129; in the left of the photo is the nose section.

Girder section from the photo below; the photo shows the complicated design work required for this relatively simple part – a joint, for example, was much more complex. All of the design work had to be accomplished without the aid of computers, something that is scarcely imaginable now.

Assembling a ring cross center-section with attachment point for the axial catwalk.

The framework of LZ 129 from behind looking towards the cruciform tail; the tail cone is still missing.

Shell and Lifting Gas Cells

The outer shell consisted of different cotton or linen fabrics of the lightest possible weight, depending on the type of load. It gave the ship its aerodynamic shape and, in particular, protected the gas cells from external influences. Several coats of Zellon were used to weatherproof the panels. In the upper areas of the ship they also received a red protective finish against ultraviolet rays. The addition of aluminum powder to the paint caused the outer skin to reflect sunlight, reducing heat buildup. Reinforcements were installed in the area of the propellers to prevent anything slung away by them, for example pieces of ice, from piercing the ship's fuselage. The sixteen gas cells in the interior were so cut so that, when full, they completely filled the available space. The two

nose and two tail cells were connected to each other, while all of the cells between them were single cells. There was a corresponding total of fourteen automatic overpressure valves plus two manually operated maneuvering valves. The valves were arranged above the axial catwalk. Between each two cells there was a vertical gas shaft running the entire height of the ship, into which the valves discharged. The gas shafts vented through ducts atop the fuselage. To assist ventilation, the lower part of the outer hull was pervious to air. For the eventual possibility of using non-flammable helium gas, the installation of additional smaller cells was possible. In this case the expensive helium would have been fed into the outer cells and the cheaper hydrogen gas into the airship's inner cells.

Test filling of a gas cell.

Engines and Electrical System

The engine nacelles were suspended in pairs from the sides of the fuselage and braced against it. They were spacious enough to allow maintenance work and, to a certain extent, repairs to be carried out. Diesel fuel was pumped from tanks near the keel walkway into gravity tanks. It could also be transferred into other tanks to trim the ship. Fuel capacity was 60,000 liters.

It was envisaged that there would be an equipment room and a switch room inside the body of the ship, accessible via a passageway extending outwards from the keel structure or on the ground by means of a trapdoor. The electrical system consisted of two machine units, one of which was used to provide additional power or as a backup. There were two 30 kW generators powered by two 40 to 50 HP (29 to 36 kW) diesel engines, plus a transformer, a storage battery system and a provision for connection to the airship hangar net. Onboard there were a total of 190 incandescent lamps with a capacity of 15 to 60 W at 220 V. A 24-Volt network fed the emergency lighting system and the signal and instrument lighting. The main grid fed all other electricity consumers, such as motors for antenna winches, stove, refrigerator, and other cooking equipment, service lift, transformer for the radio equipment, etc.

In the "tailor's shop" panels for the outer fabric shell are made.

Installing the outer shell and applying the protective finish.

The tail section is nearing completion.

One of the four Daimler diesel engines that powered the LZ 129 Hindenburg.

Aft engine gondola on the starboard side; the machinists reached their workstations from the interior of the ship by way of a catwalk.

Control Systems

The command gondola was nine meters long and measured 2.5 meters at its widest point. The control room was at the front, and behind it the map room and the rearwards-facing direction finding room. Under the gondola there was a freely rotating landing wheel. The tail control surfaces were operated from the steering room by control cables. Control forces were such that these could be operated manually by the

The radio room in LZ 129 Hindenburg.

Despite the huge size of the ship the passenger cabins were cramped and spartan.

The electric generator room.

Radio compartment; at the desk is Ober-Funkinspektor Will Speck, who was killed in the Lakehurst accident.

forwards-facing horizontal control operator or the rearwards-facing vertical control operator, although an electric motor could also be engaged. If necessary, the control surfaces could be operated from auxiliary control positions in the ventral fin. Automatic lateral control was also possible by means of the gyro compass. The ballast system was capable of either releasing water immediately in emergency situations or more slowly during normal flight operations. The moment ballast was accommodated in four fabric containers, called "trousers," in the nose and tail, each with a capacity of 500 liters. To the right and left of the keel walkway there were thirteen ballast tanks each containing 2,500 liters and two with a contents of 2,000 liters. They were operated by the vertical control operator, with the control wires running to a ballast control panel. Also located at the vertical control position was the control panel for the manually-operated gas valves. At the horizontal control position there was a magnetic compass and a repeater compass of the gyro compass system, which was connected to the electric power system.

Other equipment used in steering the ship was found in the command gondola: airspeed indicator, sonic altimeter, rpm indicators, temperature and moisture indicators, clocks, etc. It was envisaged that a device would be installed to display the holding force when the ship was anchored. Inside the ship there were twenty-four telephones and a pneumatic post system.

From the navigation room a ladder led up into a sluice room, from where one could reach the interior of the ship and the radio room. Radio equipment consisted of a short wave and a long wave transmitter each with 200 W antenna power, two so-called multiband receivers and a DF set. In a room opposite, mail was processed during flight. A small engineering room located amidships near the electrical power system, with a variety of technical equipment, completed the ship's control systems. There was also a small workshop with workbench, vise, etc., plus several compartments with spare parts spread throughout the ship.

LZ 129 Hindenburg during a test flight in March 1936.

The Passenger Compartments

Placing the passenger compartments in the interior of the ship made it possible to provide large spaces for these. The space for passenger accommodation was modest in relation to the total volume of the ship and could not compare with what was offered by steam ships, which was due to the immense amount of space required by the lifting gas. Nevertheless, accommodations were much more comfortable than on LZ 127. There were two decks, one above the other. In the larger upper deck there were twenty-five sleeping cabins in the middle, each with a floor space of 3.5m^2 for the two people that could be accommodated on long flights. Of course more people could be carried on day trips. The beds were arranged one above the other, and, during the day or when not needed, the upper one could be folded out of the way. Each cabin had a small folding washbasin with hot and cold running water, wardrobe niche with curtain, folding table and folding stool plus ladder for the upper bunk. The passenger cabins were artificially ventilated and heated with warm air, which was produced by the engine coolant. They were also connected to an electric call system. By day there were relatively spacious lounges on the same deck. A dining room was located on a 14x4 meter surface on the port side parallel to a lobby, capable of accommodating half the ship's passengers when it was fully loaded. On the starboard side, apart from an identical lobby there was a lounge with a much-admired Blüthner grand piano made of aluminum and a reading and writing room with free access to the lobby. From the lobbies one had a view downwards through sloped windows. The lower deck was reached via stairs at the end of the cabin section. Located there was a smoking cabin, over-pressurized for safety reasons, which could only be reached via a bar and was watched over by a steward at all times. Also in the lower deck was the first-

Different table arrangements in LZ 129 Hindenburg's dining room, shown to demonstrate its size; nevertheless only about half of the passengers could be fed at one time.

The promenade on LZ 129 Hindenburg's starboard side; this is a posed scene.

The food and wine offered on the Hindenburg were highly praised and compared with that served in a first-class hotel.

The smoking room on LZ 129 Hindenburg was an innovation, for otherwise smoking on board airships was as strictly forbidden as it was in airship hangars or even near airships.

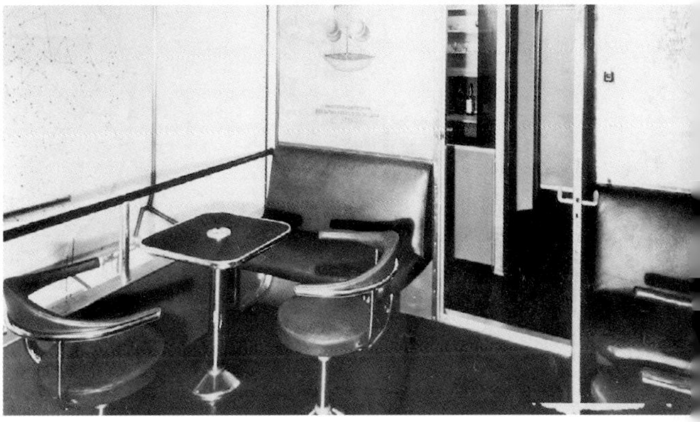

Reading and writing room for passengers on the starboard promenade.

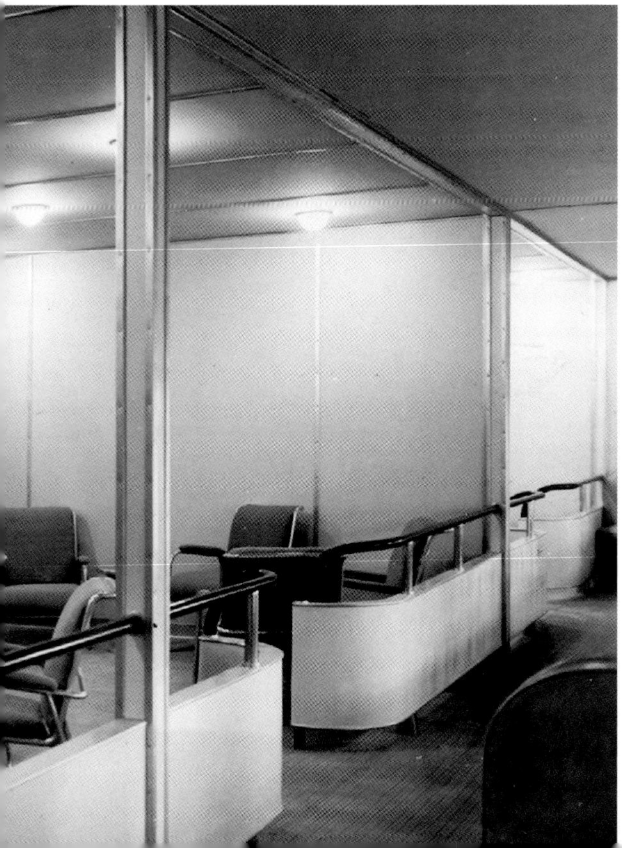

The cooks on the Hindenburg did outstanding work in their electric galley.

A journalist with secretary on board LZ 129 Hindenburg.

LZ 129 Hindenburg is brought out of the assembly hangar in Friedrichshafen.

The airship on the mobile anchor mast in Friedrichshafen-Löwenthal.

The Hindenburg's lounge with the famous aluminum Lüthner grand piano beneath the obligatory picture of Hitler (staged scene).

LZ 129 Hindenburg's command gondola; the arrangement gave the crew a view in all directions – except upwards (below).

The airships LZ 129 Hindenburg (front) and LZ 127 Graf Zeppelin over the Brandenburg Gate in Berlin, 1936.

LZ 129 over Friedrichshafen-Löwenthal; the people in the foreground give some idea of the airship hangar's size.

LZ 129 Hindenburg was a sensation and every opportunity to see it was exploited.

aid station, below it a shower that could be used with prior reservation, plus the kitchen with adjoining rooms and the officer's mess, which was connected to the kitchen by a hatch. Apart from the captain, there were special accommodations for the officers. Tent-like sleeping cabins for the crew were distributed throughout the entire ship. There was a simple lounge and washing facilities for the crew, plus baggage compartments for about ten tons of freight, which could be even more depending on the loading of the ship. Some of the cargo compartments were reached by detaching the outer hull and bracing in that area. This ends the description of LZ 129 *Hindenburg* based on Ernst Wilhelm Dörr (1936).[83]

This staged scene was part of an advertisement for trans-Atlantic airship travel.

One must realize that the available space for passengers was extremely modest aboard this huge "hotel in the sky." The dining room, lounge and writing room, smoking room and bar together covered barely 200m², so that when all the beds were occupied there was less than 4m² per passenger. While the corridor decorated as a bar promised gentlemanly travel, with a floor area of not even 4.5m² it could only offer relaxation to a fraction of the passengers.

In 1936 the Nazis requested the Deutsche Zeppelin-Reederei to send LZ 127 Graf Zeppelin (above) and LZ 129 Hindenburg over large German cities in formation to drop propaganda leaflets.

The Lakehurst Disaster

After the completion of LZ 129, in Friedrichshafen they believed that they had come a significant step closer to the realization of world airship travel. Unfortunately it was to turn out very differently. LZ 129 was wrecked in a terrible accident in Lakehurst on 6 May 1937. Everything had begun so promisingly. Hans von Schiller wrote: "The year 1936 was a complete success for the German Zeppelin line. The 'Graf' had thirteen flights to South America behind it when we returned to homeport for the winter off-season on 1 December. One week later LZ 129 *Hindenburg* also ended the travel season. The route to Rio had been travelled a total of nineteen times, the North Atlantic had been crossed ten times. The two ships had flown 500,000 kilometers. The South American service alone had transported 1,006 passengers, 9,252kg of mail and 9,198kg of freight – including an automobile and two aircraft – to Rio. In the process requests for passages and the carriage of mail and freight had risen in a steep curve. The ships were not only sold out, often passengers often had to be turned away for lack of space. The trend was therefore very positive. A third airship was supposed to enter service the next year."[84]

After the winter break, during which the airships were overhauled, it turned out that LZ 127 was still in such good condition that they believed they could continue operating it for another three years. On 16 March 1937, LZ 129 opened the new travel season under the command of *Kapitän* Max Pruss, who had commanded the ship several times in 1936, instead of Max Lehmann, who was busy with organizational tasks for the LZ and world air traffic. Hans von Schiller had been selected for the *Hindenburg*'s sister ship LZ 130 and therefore went along on several flights by LZ 129. He was enthusiastic, because it handled much better than LZ 127. To him, as to First Officer Albert Sammt, LZ 129 was a "dream ship."[85,86] It had been to the USA ten times in 1936. Eighteen trips to the United States were planned for 1937, and instead of remaining there one or two days, it was planned to initiate the return flight the same day it arrived. Only thus could such a tight schedule have been maintained.

On 3 May 1937 LZ 129 took off on its first trip of that year to the States, the ship's sixty-seventh flight in total. The arrival of a Zeppelin always drew large crowds to Lakehurst. Although the weather was less than cooperative, this time the numbers were especially large, for they had long been deprived of the spectacle. A storm front made it seem advisable to postpone the landing. The ship flew a wide loop and waited until the ground station in Lakehurst, which was commanded by Charles E. Rosendahl, signaled that weather conditions were suitable for landing. And then the catastrophe happened.

The report by the German investigating committee was certainly one of the most objective written about the *Hindenburg* disaster. The chapter "Execution of the Landing and the Fire" clearly laid out the many problems that afflicted large airship travel, independent of the special problems at Lakehurst; this had been expressed in many reports over other flights in which Zeppelins had gotten into trouble, only this time there were fatal consequences. The report, signed by Dr. Hugo Eckener, Dr. Ludwig Dürr, the airship captains Breithaupt and Bock and the scientists Diekmann and Hoffmann, declared the following: "... When the ship approached Lakehurst Station from the west-southwest at a height of 200 meters, the ceiling over the station was 600 to 900 meters and light rain was falling. The sky did, however, show signs of clearing to the west. Barometric pressure was 755mm Hg, the air temperature 16° C, the relative humidity 98%, the surface wind was light and variable. On its first pass over the field ... the airship's officers realized that the crew on the ground were positioned for a landing into an east wind, and that the approach would have to be made from over the anchor mast west of the airfield. The airship therefore made a wide arc five to six miles from the field and then approached the landing mast from that direction. As the wind had since shifted to the southeast, the airship swung out to port to approach into the wind and, after completing this second turn, approached the mast from a northerly direction. ... While executing this wide turn, about ten minutes before the landing ropes were dropped, gas was released from Cells 4 to 14 for fifteen seconds.

LZ 129 Hindenburg over the landing field in Lakehurst just before the accident on 6 May 1937; in the foreground is the mobile landing mast.

As the ship was tail heavy, before and during the final turn gas was again released from the forward five cells, twice for fifdteen seconds and once for five seconds. For the same reason, water was released three times from Ring 77, a total of 1,100kg. After the first big turn was completed, the engines were reduced to idle ahead. During the approach in the final turn, several minor maneuvers were undertaken with the engines. About two minutes before the nose anchor ropes were dropped, all engines were run at full reverse power for a duration of about one minute. Then the forward engines went to idle ahead and the aft engines to idle. The engines remained in this position until the end, except for a brief period of 'full ahead' on the forward engines. ... Because of the ship's tail-heaviness, during the landing approach six men had been sent from the middle of the ship to the nose in order to trim the ship nose-heavy. At the moment the forward landing ropes were dropped, the command gondola was ninety meters above sea level, or about sixty meters above the ground. First the starboard anchor rope was dropped, followed immediately by the port anchor rope. As the ship began drifting to the west, the port anchor rope was immediately attached to the rope of the anchor rope pickup truck, which then tightened sharply while the starboard rope was held by the landing party. The main nose cable, which was used to attach the ship to the anchor mast, had been lowered about fifteen meters and was thus still far from the ground at the moment that the fire broke out. The toggles on Ring 62 had also been lowered. When the fire broke out the standard ladder on Ring 47 had just been released and had come down just a few meters. Immediately before the

The fire spread from the tail in seconds; because the fire caused the ship to lose lift, water ballast tanks – visible beneath the ship – were spontaneously opened.

fire broke out, a witness observed ... a fluttering of the outer skin on the upper port side between Rings 62 and 77, which enclosed Cell No.5. As the ship was not moving and the propeller thrust had to pass far below the fluttering spot, this undulation of the outer skin may possibly have been caused by gas emanating from a cell. At 13:25, about four minutes after the landing ropes fell, the fire broke out at the tail of the ship. Statements as to where the fire started in some cases vary widely. The reason for this lies on the one hand in the rapid spread of the fire itself, on the other in the different vantage points from which the observers watched as the ship landed, and the large physical size of the airship which made an overall view much more difficult. After evaluating the witness statements from this aspect, the conclusion was reached that the first fire broke out on the topside of the ship, specifically in front of the leading edge of the vertical stabilizer above Cells 4 and 5. From there, in the space of about fifteen seconds it spread forwards about twenty to thirty meters, until the first explosion took place. About half a minute passed between the initial outbreak of the fire and the main body of the ship striking the ground."

The report confirmed statements by expert witnesses, according to which, "the landing of the airship was carried out entirely properly and ... the conduct of the crew before and during the disaster was exemplary." There is also nothing to suggest that the ship was not in perfect condition. The remains of the totally destroyed airship provided no clues as to the cause of the accident. All that remains, therefore, is speculation, which ranges from sabotage to pilot error. The report favored the pilot error theory in that it characterized as dangerous reversing the ship while simultaneously venting hydrogen gas under the existing atmospheric conditions with high electrostatic charge. Immediately after the Lakehurst disaster, Eckener spontaneously issued an "edict" prescribing to airship commanders exactly how to act in similar situations. The accident

The Hindenburg sinks to the ground tail first. The burning airship was only about 200 meters from the landing mast. Right: The American ground handling team runs for their lives.

claimed the lives of thirty-six people – thirteen passengers, twenty-two crewmembers and one member of the American ground crew. Among the dead was Dipl.Ing. Ernst Lehmann, who like several others died soon after the tragedy as a result of severe burns. Miraculously, sixty-two of those on board survived the disaster.

Stunned helpers in front of the smoldering, smoking wreckage that was left of the airship; thirteen passengers, twenty-two crewmembers and one member of the groundcrew lost their lives. An American military honor guard in front of the remains of LZ 129 Hindenburg (below).

No Solution to the Helium Problem

After this accident it was obvious that hydrogen-filled airships could no longer be used to carry passengers. After arriving in Friedrichshafen, LZ 127, which at the time of the disaster was on its way home from South America, was taken out of service. The Zeppelin airship makers immediately tried to convert LZ 130, then under construction, for the use of helium, as it was assumed that the Americans would now be ready to provide the precious gas. Despite the shock of the accident, they were not idle, for just one week later the Secretary of the Interior Ickes presented to the cabinet in Washington a request from Germany for almost 300,000m^3 of helium gas for LZ 130. President Roosevelt,[87] who was sympathetic to Eckener and his world airship idea, turned the matter over to a special advisory committee. After a few days it decided that the USA should sell helium for use in commercial airship traffic between the United Sates and other countries, and on 25 May it passed this recommendation on to the president.

While there were fears that helium-filled ships might find military use in case of conflict, humanitarian considerations prevailed, "in order to promote economy and science, lessen human suffering and strengthen international friendship."[88] Roosevelt supported the proposal and placed it in the hands of the responsible committee of congress. During hearings, Dr. Eckener stressed to the committee the pointlessness of using airships in a military role. Things seemed to be going well.

On 7 December 1937 the German embassy in Washington telegraphed Berlin that the requested quantity of helium had been approved and that the remaining export questions were mere formalities. Gas cylinders were transported to the port of Galveston, Texas to be filled with liquid helium. The first load was ready to ship at the end of 1938. It should be noted that the production, delivery and transport of such huge quantities required an enormous technical and logistical effort and it was unlikely that the total quantity would be on hand in Friedrichshafen before the end of the year. Furthermore it would not have been sufficient for the initial filling of the ship, as shown by figures calculated by Luftschiffbau Zeppelin the year before: "Calculation of the helium requirements for LZ 130, assuming fifteen to twenty-five round trips in 1937, meaning from Frankfurt to Lakehurst and back, was based on the following consumption estimates.

First 200,000m^3 was necessary for filling the ship, about 530,000m^3 was estimated for losses through diffusion during the flight there and back and during the stopover in Lakehurst and for cleaning, etc. The necessary total quantity was thus 730,000m^3."[89]

This estimate caused those responsible considerable headaches with respect to financing, but there was no other choice if they wanted to resume passenger services. But then the situation was overtaken by events. Hitler annexed Austria on 12 March 1938, and the good relations with the USA that Eckener had worked so hard to build abruptly collapsed. Just two days later a deputy in the House of Representatives introduced a draft bill for the purpose of cancelling the export approval granted a few months earlier. Despite his efforts, Eckener was unable to change the mind of the American government and so he was forced "to come to the conclusion that Hitler had dug the grave of Zeppelin travel."[90]

On 14 September 1938 LZ 130 Graf Zeppelin II was brought out of the hangar for its first flight. The airship, which was outwardly recognizable by its tractor propellers, never entered passenger service.

The Last Hope: LZ 130

LZ 130 was the last big airship ever built, however relatively little attention has been paid to it in the extensive Zeppelin literature. The reason for this may be as follows: because it was filled with hydrogen gas, LZ 130 could not carry passengers. It made several flights on missions leading up to the war and was used for propaganda purposes by the Nazis, but it was not popular like its immediate predecessors. After it was grounded in autumn 1939 at the start of the Second World War, for a short time the ship could be seen in Frankfurt, but in

Popular illustration of LZ 130's particulars in a brochure produced by the Deutsche Zeppelin-Reederei GmbH. Even after the Hindenburg disaster, it was used to advertise airship flights, even though it was already clear that no helium would be received from the USA. The brochure promised travelers "Reliability, fast and comfortable travel, every amenity and comfort." It declared that the impressions of a Zeppelin trip were "deep and varied" – as if Lakehurst hadn't happened.

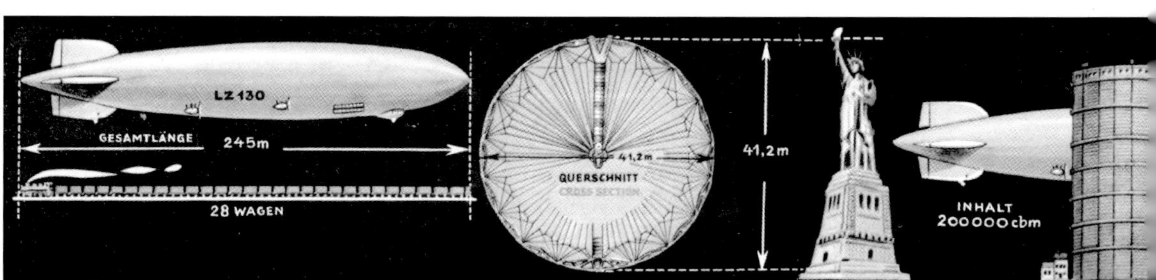

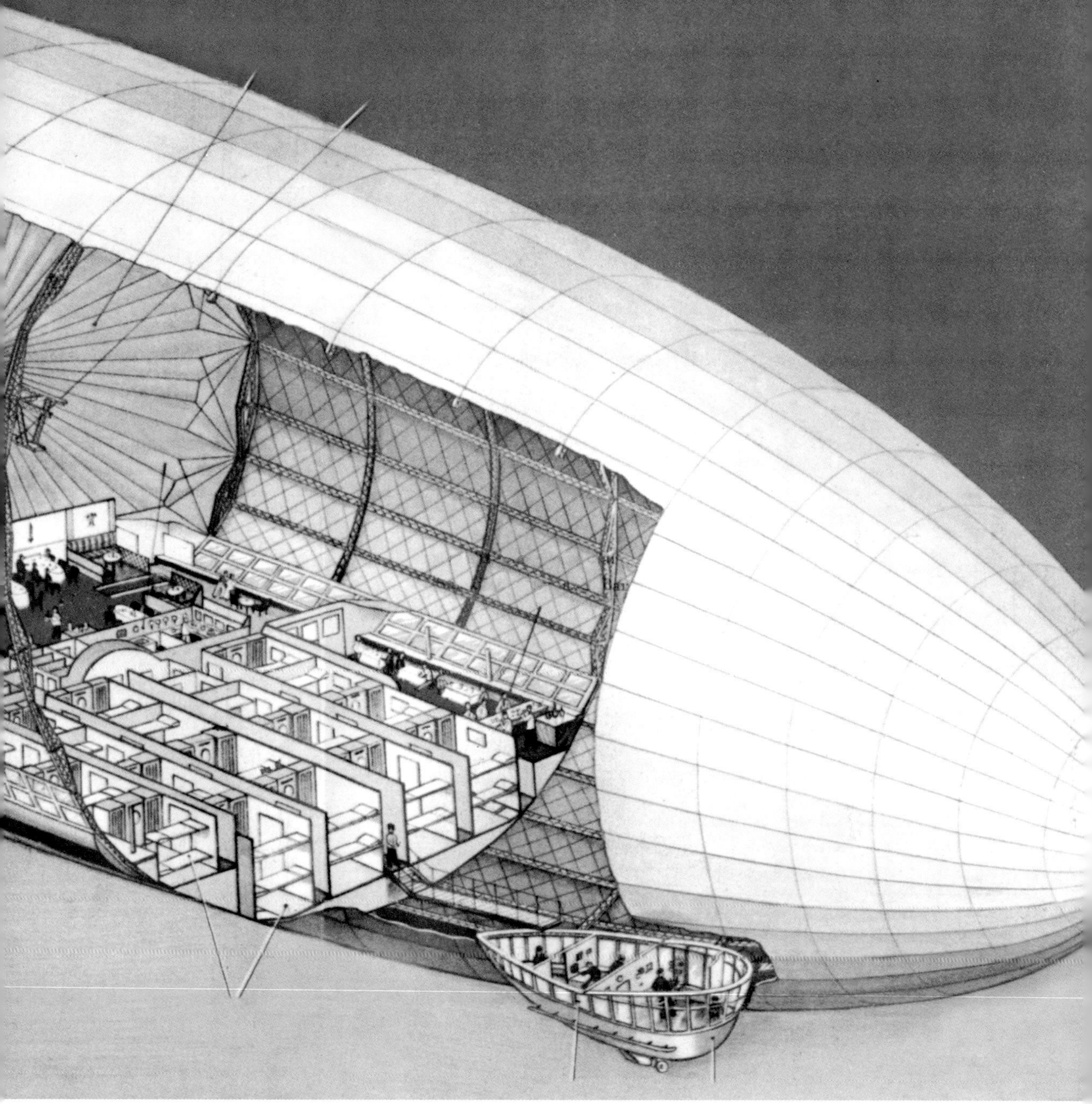

200 000 KILO
LÄNGE DER GERIPPETRÄGER ca. 22 KILOMETER
VERWENDETE NIETEN ca. 5,5 MILLIONEN
LÄNGE DES STAHLDRAHTES ca. 135 KILOMETER
FLÄCHE DES ZELLSTOFFES ca. 56 000 QUADRATMETER

spring 1940 it and LZ 127 were scrapped and the aluminum sent to the armaments industry.

LZ 130 marked the end of the roughly forty-year history of the Zeppelin airship travel. Construction began in June 1936. Based on experience gained with hydrogen ships in recent years and because helium was not available, LZ 130 was also designed to be carried aloft by hydrogen. The framework was already complete when LZ 129 crashed, which is why it remained unchanged. W.E. Dörr wrote: "Those passenger fittings that had been installed were removed. The layout was changed with respect to the arrangement of the compartments to one another ... and at the same time installations were reduced to accommodate forty passengers. Through this and a number of less obvious measures, we were able to reduce the weight of the ship body. This was important with respect to the intended use of helium as a lifting gas, as this gas is significantly heavier than hydrogen gas, which, given the size of the ship, results in a loss in tare weight on the order of about twenty tons."[91] Some of the passenger cabins were designed to have outer windows, which was supposed to make air travel even more attractive. Like LZ 129, LZ 130 was 245 meters long, had a maximum diameter of 41.2 meters and a filled gas capacity of 200,000m^3. Maximum height on the landing wheels was 44.1 meters, maximum width, measured over the propellers, 46.8 meters. To further save weight, the tail surfaces were reduced by 0.6 meters compared to LZ 129. Like LZ 129, it was powered by four Daimler diesel engines with a combined output of 4,200 HP (3087 kW). Unlike LZ 129, the propellers were arranged as tractor units. The engine nacelles were much bigger and also differed in shape. Dörr: "The reason for this was the installation of a new ballast water collection system. This reduced or almost eliminated the consumption of lifting gas caused by the need to equalize the weight lost through fuel consumption during flight by venting lifting gas. Now water captured by cooling and condensing the engine exhaust replaced the weight of the consumed fuel. Multistage cooling systems within the nacelles were envisaged for this purpose and the cooling air would be forced into the gondola by the propeller now located at the front of the gondola and out the rear end again."[92]

When it was learned with certainty that no helium could be expected from the USA, several modifications once again had to be made to the ship. LZ 130 made a total of just thirty flights[93] before it was grounded – of course without private, paying passengers.

Construction work on LZ 131, which was supposed to be essentially similar to its predecessor, proceeded only as far as several rings. With the same diameter, the ship was to have had a length of 260 meters and, with a gas volume of 223,000m^3, was to have been capable of transporting 80 to 100 passengers. One main ring and two auxiliary rings provided the extra length. Work on the airship was halted when the war broke out.

Attempts to Retrieve the Past

"The detection of mines ... is a central problem in the resettlement of former crisis and war zones." Thus began a press release[1] by the Zeppelin-Luftschifftechnik GmbH of Friedrichshafen, which had been test-flying the prototype of a "Zeppelin NT"[2] since 1997 in order to obtain a type certification from the German Federal Civil Aeronautics Administration. To the Institute for High-Frequency Technology at the German Center for Aviation and Space Travel (DLR) in Oberpfaffenhofen near Munich, the airship seemed the "ideal platform with which to achieve this objective." The team had "developed several sensors that were capable of taking over important subtasks in mine clearing, including a microwave radiometer, whose

Framework of the Zeppelin NT (production airship SN 02) in the hangar in Friedrichshafen.

fifteen-meter-long antenna was supposed to register the inherent electromagnetic radiation of a mine." This huge expenditure was certainly worthwhile, for every mine that was detected meant human lives saved.

The prospect of this task brought a clearly audible sigh of relief from the Friedrichshafen airship builders, for until then their target groups had been more or less restricted to the areas of tourism and advertising. They had prognosticated scientific and monitoring tasks as possible fields of operation, but exactly what this meant had gotten no further than general suggestions. Now the task was finally concrete, it had defined a human concern and would, provided it was feasible, spur the ZLT team to optimize the airship specifically for this mission, which would then also benefit other fields.

The Zeppelin NT is an ambitious project that was born in Friedrichshafen. Understandably, the call for a new Zeppelin had never died out in the city. After the Second World War a group of former Luftschiffbau Zeppelin technicians and aircrew produced a study directly linked to the final Zeppelins and which consequently was to have been called the LZ 132.[3] The project was nothing more than the continuation of the LZ 131, construction of which began before the war but was never completed. Of course it was doomed to fail, because it was based on unrealistic conditions and offered no significant improvements.

For a long time the engineers were unable to detach themselves from the idea of a rigid airship

Framework joints, the girder (foreground) and transverse bulkhead are joined together.

View of the hangar, which is also used as an assembly hall: framework (left) and shell for a production airship, which has been inflated for test purposes (center); servicing the prototype Zeppelin NT (right).

Zeppelin NT on the mobile anchor mast at the airfield in Friedrichshafen (above and below).

with all the principal features of the Zeppelins. In particular, the framework structure remained virtually identical everywhere. In England in the 1980s there was a project with the obvious designation LZ 133, but with no contact with the former Luftschiffbau in Friedrichshafen, like almost all such projects worldwide, it came to nothing. Even if there was no support in the area of design or even – as was always hoped – finance, they at least expected moral support. They always found an advocate in that city. Out of conviction, someone was always ready to pass often bizarre plans to the city, which administered the Zeppelin Fund, and profusely explain the often confused ideas about the future of the new airship. By closed-mindedly clinging to hopelessly obsolete models, the

Port propeller in ground position.

inventors overlooked the fact that future almost always meant the past laboriously brought into the present. But as Friedrichshafen had to administer, not just a spiritual, but more importantly a financial legacy, which could not be jeopardized, the inventors were patiently put off. The policy of putting off, delaying was used successfully and even paid off, for the name "Zeppelin" remained on everyone's lips. Only in recent times was a value placed on the level of awareness of the name, which captured a leading place worldwide.[4] Consequently, at some point they had to consider seriously and fundamentally grappling with the theme of the airship and not leave it to outsiders. Admittedly, in the 1970s and 1980s conditions were not conducive to tackling the future of the airship. An example of this was the so-called Helitruck, a hybrid vehicle that was supposed to combine the features of the helicopter, aircraft and rigid airship.[5] It failed in the development phase, not least because the project was tackled halfheartedly. Nevertheless, it showed the public that there was still interest in house. Meanwhile the Helitruck disappeared quietly and without fanfare.

The beginnings of the Zeppelin NT, which go back to the late-1980s, were initially greeted with skepticism, because as with all other projects it immediately began with grandiose announcements. Market figures were projected, schedules for first flights published, fantastic prognoses for the future were made, a flying model was quasi-praised

View of the passenger and control gondola of the prototype Zeppelin NT (advertising photo).

as a completed Zeppelin airship which only had to be built. With such unprofessional assessments, the optimistic deadlines could not be met, and the project threatened to fail because of mismanagement. Meanwhile euphoria had given way to a more sober way of thinking. The Zeppelin-Luftschifftechnik GmbH, which had been formed expressly for the further development of the project, was restructured. New management with experience in aviation technology dialed back expectations to a realistic level, and the grandiose announcements gave way to more sober and solid public relations.

Meanwhile, what was being shown was not an actual Zeppelin, characterized by a rigid framework enclosing the gas cells and an outer pressure-free shell, but instead a semi-rigid airship which retained its outer shape through internal pressure supported by ballonets. One innovation was a supporting structure in the interior of the shell with three girders of aluminum and twelve triangle-shaped transverse bulkheads made of carbon-fiber-reinforced plastic. This system was recognized as patent-worthy in Germany and abroad. "The weatherproof shell, a multi-layer laminate of Tedlar foil and polyester fabric, is attached to this framework throughout, so that all of the attacking aerodynamic forces and lift are transmitted directly to the supporting structure. All external components, such as engines, gondola, tail surfaces with elevators and rudder, are joined to the supporting structure."[6]

What has elevated the air vehicle to Zeppelin status is the fact that it was developed within the Zeppelin group of companies. With a length of seventy-five meters and a maximum diameter of 14.2 meters, it has a gas volume of 8,225m^3; the maximum ballonet volume is given as 1,805m^3. Propulsion is provided by three much-tested and reliable Lycoming engines, each producing 200 HP (147 kW). One engine on each side is equipped with a 120° upwards-swiveling propeller. The third engine is located in the center of the tail and powers a pusher propeller, which can swivel downwards by 90°. By means of a connectible transmission it can also drive a sideways-acting propeller to move the airship about its yaw axis. All of the propeller blades can be set from forward to reverse thrust by the pilot. This arrangement gives, "... the LZ N07[7] a level of maneuverability previously unheard of in an airship. This will minimize the general shortcoming of wind sensitivity by airships at low speed. Purely theoretically, the Zeppelin NT should even be able to get by without a ground crew. In addition, the NT invalidates the lighter than air principle, for at takeoff the Zeppelin can have up to 500kg 'excess weight'. Despite this, by means of the upwards-directed propellers the airship can lift off vertically."[8] Claimed maximum speed is 130 kph, cruising speed 115 kph. For sightseeing operations, the NT can carry a crew of two and twelve passengers. While there will be no revival of large airship operations, it is likely that certain market niches can be filled. It is doubtful, however that the product will meet the purely commercial interests of its future operators, for whom the above-mentioned humanitarian missions or research purposes play no role. It is all too easy to forget that weather may restrict operations to a relatively few days per year, that a suitable landing place and a sturdy landing mast must be available at each destination and an airship hangar at its home base at least. A "certain potential" is seen for such airships, "however, one also needs the infrastructure of an airline and a corresponding market. Only when the two come together will the airship program have a future."[9,10]

Zeppelin "Relatives"

Schütte-Lanz, the Only German Competitor

Very few inventors and designers dared tackle the rigid airship. It is significant that, with one exception, no German industrialist took up the challenge, which promised money and fame, and seized the idea of the rigid airship. The Zeppelin airship was in fact entirely capable of further development, but obviously Zeppelin's failures were a powerful deterrent. And so Johann Schütte was Zeppelin's only competition in Germany. The naval architect had recognized the weak spots of the Zeppelin design, and after the Echterdingen accident in 1908 he developed his own airship, which differed from the Zeppelin airship in several significant aspects. Together with the mechanical engineer Lanz, in 1909 he began building airships in Mannheim-Rheinau. From the beginning, thanks to their aerodynamic shape the Schütte-Lanz airships, which bore the designation SL, had better handling characteristics than the cylindrical and therefore easier to manufacture early Zeppelins. This despite the fact that, in the long run, its framework of plywood ribs could not compete with the aluminum structure of the Zeppelin.

The war also benefited development at Schütte-Lanz. Total production of SL airships reached twenty-two by 1918. The last reached a length of more than 198 meters and, with a maximum diameter of just under twenty-three meters, had a gas volume of 56,300m^3. As this subject is very extensive, the reader is referred to the writings of Johann Schütte and, as previously mentioned, the works of Dorothea Haaland, who described in detail this interesting chapter in aviation history. Henry Cord Meyer examined it from a political point of view as he did the Zeppelin airship company. Outside Germany, operational rigid airships based on the Zeppelin system were only built in the USA and in England, and these will be examined briefly. The main reason why the airship failed to spread worldwide is probably the enormous cost of the airships themselves and their ground organization, especially the vital hangars. The cost to performance ratio was unconvincing. As well, there was the high accident rate and the shortage of non-flammable helium gas, which was only available in quantities worth mentioning in the USA, whose government treated it as a monopoly.

American Zeppelins

News of the flights by the first Zeppelin airship in 1900 of course reached America and made the count well known there. Especially in the larger cities, German clubs, in particular veterans associations, German newspapers and the aero clubs, which like everywhere else in the world were springing up out of the ground, followed the activities on Lake Constance with enthusiasm. LZ 4's accident at Echterdingen in 1908 also evoked much sympathy in the USA, for too many German-Americans Graf Zeppelin had become a symbolic figure of their former homeland. Honors in the form of honorary memberships, invitations and letters of thanks for "service to the Fatherland" were quite common. Initially, however, the First World War prevented close contacts, which would have been welcomed because of the count's plans to establish an airship service between the two continents.

ZR 1 Shenandoah at the tall mast in Lakehurst.

ZR 1 *Shenandoah*

A not entirely desired exchange with the USA took place during the First World War, when LZ 96 (L 49) fell into French hands virtually intact.[1] The ship was disassembled and measured. After the war the *Shenandoah*[2] was built in the USA based on the LZ 96 plans. It was the USA's first rigid airship, was filled with helium and received the type designation ZR 1.[3] The ship was 207 meters long (LZ 96 196.5m), had a diameter of 24.1 meters (23.93m) and a lifting gas volume of about 60,800m³ (55,800m³). Peter Kleinheins described it as follows: "ZR 1 was more powerfully built than the fair weather, high-altitude airship L 49; at thirty-eight tons its own weight was forty-four percent greater, its payload of twenty-two tons forty-five percent less. ZR 1 was powered by six (later five) Packard engines with a combined output of 1,800 HP [1,320 kW] (later 1,500 HP [1,100 kW]) and had a speed of 110 kph [95 kph]. L 49 had reached 108 kph at higher altitude on 1,200 HP [880 kW]. Externally, ZR 1 differed little from the last Zeppelins. Ballast water extraction devices were suspended above the engine gondolas and their drag resulted in a speed loss of several meters per second. In the summer of 1924 the forward engine gondola was replaced by a radio compartment as an extension of the command gondola. To minimize the possible loss of helium, the number of overpressure valves was reduced to ten for the twenty cells; the cells were connected by a balancing line."[4]

The ship was used by the Americans mainly for familiarization with large airships. It anchored at a tall mast or – a real innovation – a mast on the airship tender *Patoka*, a converted tanker. ZR 1 made a cross-country publicity flight, introducing the airship to Americans and promoting the construction of large airships, for the planned building program had many critics in the Congress and the navy. When it returned to Lakehurst, ZR 3 *Los Angeles* was in the hangar, having completed a much-celebrated crossing of the Atlantic. Because the hydrogen gas absolutely had to be replaced with helium, but not enough was available, much was taken from ZR 1, which meant that the *Shenandoah* was grounded for half a year. On 2 September 1925 ZR 1 took off on another demonstration flight, which ended in disaster the following day. Over the state of Ohio, the airship broke up in a storm with heavy turbulence. Part of the ship came down like a free balloon and because of its helium filling there was no fire. Because of this twenty-nine of the crew of forty-three survived.[5,6] The crash of ZR 1 was a severe

ZR 3 Los Angeles in Lakehurst.

setback for American airship aviation, which was preparing to realize grand plans.

ZR 3 *Los Angeles*

ZR 3 remained in service for years and survived a number of difficult situations, which was due to its solid construction at the expense of performance and payload. Kleinheins described a situation that failed to result in serious consequences only because of this construction: "As it so often was, on 25 August 1927 it [ZR 3 *Los Angeles*] was anchored at the forty-nine-meter-high mast in Lakehurst. Then something unsettling happened: a strong breeze came from the sea in the opposite direction of the previous light wind. It blew under the tail and raised it until the ship was vertical with its nose on the mast. After some time it dropped slowly and gracefully into a horizontal position on the other side. None of the twenty-five men on board was injured; the only damage was caused by loose parts that fell along the gangway to the nose of the ship. That day the ultimate decision was made against the technique of anchoring at a tall mast."[7] And an example of the Americans' willingness to experiment: "On 27 January 1928 an impressive and successful experiment was undertaken. ZR 3 landed on the deck of the American aircraft carrier *Saratoga*. This was the only time the airship landed on a carrier; conversely tying up at the mast of the *Patoka* had long since become routine. *Los Angeles* tied up there a total of 44 times."[8]

ZRS 4 *Akron* and ZRS 5 *Macon*

The signing of the agreement establishing the Goodyear-Zeppelin Corporation in 1923 began a new chapter in American airship aviation. A number of qualified German engineers under the direction of Karl Arnstein[9] were given the opportunity to go from Luftschiffbau Zeppelin in Friedrichshafen to Akron, Ohio and take part in the development of modern large airships. Several rigid airships were projected, but first a contract for the construction of two large airships, ZRS 4 and ZRS 5, which were envisaged for the strategic reconnaissance role, was signed with the US Navy. Small aircraft carried by the airships would reconnoiter large areas around them. ZRS 4, which was given the name *Akron*, made its maiden flight on 25 September 1931 with 113 persons on board. For its day the ship was a sensation. Not only did it break all size and performance records, but in many aspects it was so modern that it anticipated the *Hindenburg*, which appeared in the skies five years later, and indeed in some aspects surpassed it. But there was more to airship aviation than technical advancement, for handling large airships required much experience and skill. And so there was much criticism in the USA, primarily directed at the lack of experience in handling large airships – not unjustified, as events would show. They obviously wanted "too much, too soon."[10]

ZR 4 Akron was 239.3 meters long and had a maximum diameter of 40.5 meters, resulting in a maximum gas volume of just under 195,000m³.[11] The basic concept followed the Zeppelin design, but its framework, in particular, had to be modified for the use of helium gas. It was powered by eight twelve-cylinder Maybach V-engines, which together produced about 4,490 HP (3,300 kW). The engines were arranged inside the fuselage at right angles to the ship's longitudinal axis and drove two-bladed, swiveling propellers by means of five-meter-long shafts.[12] Another sensation soon followed: in October 1931 ZRS 4 made a flight with 207 persons on board, remaining aloft for ten hours.

Despite all the care with which the *Akron* had been built, it was lost on its seventy-third flight on 4 April 1933. It was off the coast of New England when it unexpectedly ran into a storm. Turbulence and rainsqualls drove it onto the water's surface. Just three of the seventy-eight crewmen were pulled from the sea alive.[13] It was the highest number of fatalities ever suffered in the crash of an airship. There was severe criticism of the lifesaving equipment carried by the airship.[14] Among the victims of ZRS 4 was Admiral William A. Moffet, one of the strongest advocates of large airship construction in the USA.

By that time ZRS 5 *Macon* was almost complete, and despite manifold reservations it made its first ascent on 21 April 1933. The ship embodied a number of improvements over ZRS

ZRS 5 Macon over Manhattan 1933-34.

4. It was capable of housing five small aircraft, as requested. They took off and landed from a retractable trapeze located in the bottom part of the fuselage.[15] The *Macon* had a payload that was 3.6 tons greater than that of the *Akron*, This was achieved through weight savings, but obviously at the cost of safety. Also noteworthy was its maximum speed of 141 kph compared to the 128 kph of the ZRS 4, the result of three-blade variable-pitch propellers, more streamlined outrigger shape for the swiveling propellers, oil coolers, etc. ZRS 5 *Macon* was moved to Sunnyvale, California in October 1933 to take part in fleet maneuvers off the west coast. In the process it did not present "a good picture, because it was deployed in a very restricted area despite being capable of long-range reconnaissance"[16] and within range of the ships' guns would have been shot down had it been the real thing.

It is difficult to understand why such missions were tested after the experiences in Europe during the First World War. In 1934 during a flight over land, the ship was caught in heavy turbulence and almost lost its port stabilizer. The weak spot was the attachment of the leading edge of the stabilizers to an auxiliary ring instead of a main ring; the auxiliary ring could not take the loads. Strengthening of the weak spot was planned.

From the navy's point of view, the months that followed produced usable results. The undercarriages of the aircraft carried by the

Macon were not needed over the ocean, therefore they were replaced by an external fuel tank which extended their range considerably, making reconnaissance operations more effective. The radio system had been so improved that the aircraft could be reliably located and guided back to the airship, even at great distances. But then the drama unfolded. Kleinheins: "On 11 February [1935] it [the *Macon*] took off on a reconnaissance mission during a fleet movement from San Diego to San Francisco. The planned reinforcements of the critical framework components of the ventral and horizontal stabilizers, carried out between flights, had been completed the previous day; they had yet to be carried out on the dorsal stabilizer. *Macon* did good work: its aircraft came and went and delivered a wealth of reports. Already on its way home to Sunnyvale, at about 19:00 on 12 February it suddenly ran into an unusually powerful squall. The dorsal stabilizer began to tear from the fuselage, broke apart and flew away; three gas cells, pierced by parts of the structure, emptied. In panic, the ship's commanders jettisoned fifteen tons of ballast in five minutes, and that settled the ship's fate. It climbed to 1,480 meters (altitude at which the lifting gas occupied the entire volume of the shell was 850m), helium discharged, and the almost eighteen-ton loss of lift allowed the ship to drop rapidly. The release of additional ballast and downwards thrust from the pivoting propellers slowed the ship's fall. It was destroyed when it struck the water, but only two of eighty-three men lost their lives."[17]

The shock was nevertheless great. After this accident even the *Los Angeles*, which was considered extremely reliable, never flew again. Until 1936 it was only used in experiments in the hangar or on the mast. ZR 3 was scrapped in 1939-40. The Zeppelin system had thus also come to an end in the USA.

English Rigid Airships

The only European country other than Germany to build a number of rigid airships was Great Britain. A total of seventeen was built using the Zeppelin principle, some in modified form. Their features and several of their fates are described in brief.[18]

Experiments during the First World War

The naval airship Navy 1 of 1911, dubbed the *Mayfly*, proved to be an unsuccessful design. It had a lifting gas capacity of 21,000m^3 but was not capable of flight because it was too heavy. Another rigid airship was not completed until the end of 1916. It was designated No.9 and its design resembled that of LZ 16, which was forced down near Lunéville, France in 1913. With a volume of 25,000m^3, No.9 was larger than LZ 16 (19,550m^3) and had swiveling propellers powered by Maybach engines built under license in England. Because of poor handling characteristics, the ship was scrapped after less than 200 flying hours. During the war the navy ordered a total of thirteen airships, some of which were not completed until after war's end. Several of these were lengthened versions of the No.9 type, however their payload was far less than that of contemporary Zeppelin airships. Not until the R 31 and R 32, which were completed near and after the end of the war respectively, were two airships available that were "successful designs."[19] With a gas capacity of 42,400m^3, they were 185 meters long and had a diameter of 19.7 meters. They had a plywood framework, however, and should therefore be compared to the Schütte-Lanz airships. This is not surprising, for in 1916 a former Schütte-Lanz employee had delivered plans to the British admiralty.[20] The next two ships, R 33 and R 34, had a gas capacity of 55,200m^3 and were similar to LZ 76, which force-landed in England in September 1916. They also incorporated improvements from LZ 96, which came down in France in 1917 and was the inspiration for ZR 1 *Shenandoah*.[21] In July 1919, R 34 made the sensational first crossing of the Atlantic. The ship was badly damaged in a storm in January 1921 and had to be scrapped. R 36 was a lengthened version (by 8.5 meters) of LZ 96, navy airship L 49, which came down near Bourbonne les Bains in 1917. It was 205 meters long with a diameter of twenty-seven meters as opposed to 23.93 meters, and its gas volume was 60,000m^3 compared to LZ 49's 55,800m^3. R 36, which was a passenger ship capable of carrying fifty passengers, was powered by three Sunbeam Cossack engines each producing 347 HP (255 kW) and two Maybach engines each producing

258 HP (190 kW). The latter had been removed from LZ 113, which had been delivered to England in July 1920 as a reparations payment. Because of its limited payload of just sixteen tons, however, R 36 was ill suited for passenger service. R 37 was not completed because of feared construction cost overruns.

R 80, which made its maiden flight on 19 July 1920, is considered a separate design. Kleinheins wrote of it: "The relatively small R 80 no longer had cylindrical fuselage sections, and with a gas volume of 34,500m³ had a payload of more than eighteen tons (almost 50% of lifting capacity). Its gondolas were circular in cross-section and displayed perfect streamlined shape. The command gondola and the forward engine nacelle directly behind it were far offset from the fuselage, while the two side gondolas were much closer. There were no engine gondolas in the rear. The nose gondola housed two Wolseley-Maybach engines each producing 231 HP (170 kW) driving a single propeller. In the side gondolas, the same engines, which were reversible, drove propellers mounted in the rear. With total power of just 925 HP (680 kW) the beautiful airship achieved a speed of 105 kph."[22]

LZ 127 Graf Zeppelin landed at the English Cardington airfield on 18 August 1931; in the background on the high mast is the British airship R 100.

England Builds Big Airships

R 38, the last of the airships ordered by the Royal Navy during the war, entered a new dimension. It flew for the first time in June 1921. With a length of 213 meters and a gas volume of 77,000m³, it was the largest rigid airship in the world and was not surpassed until 1928, when LZ 127 *Graf Zeppelin* appeared. The U.S. Navy wanted to take the ship as ZR 2. R 38 was elegant in appearance, had an acceptable payload of forty-six tons and a maximum speed of 115 kph, but the design of its framework was too weak for the desired performance, and on 24 August 1921 the ship broke up during its fourth test flight.[23] This debacle seriously dampened enthusiasm for airships in the USA, for sixteen Americans had died in the disaster.[24] While this brought an end to the British military's experimentation with airships, but the civilian sector clung to the system despite the accidents and disasters. Despite the tragic loss of R 38, in 1928 the British government ordered two new rigid airships, with the R 100 built by a private consortium and R 101 by the government's own facility. With a gas volume of 141,500m³, it was calculated that they would have a payload of sixty tons and be capable of transporting 100 passengers between England and Canada at a cruising speed of 100 kph. The level of comfort on board was to have been extraordinarily high. The private company Airship Guarantee, a Vickers subsidiary, employed the simplest possible design with a minimum of different components. R 100 was 216 meters long and had a maximum diameter of 40.5 meters, however its payload of fifty-one tons was below that demanded by the specification. The ship had only sixteen girders, which gave it its characteristic angular appearance. The three engine nacelles, each with two-blade reversible propellers, were mounted in the tail far away from the passenger area. The six engines combined to produce 3,960 HP (2,910 kW), and maximum speed was 130 kph. R 100 – like its sister ship R 101 – for the first time had all control and passenger fittings inside the airship, with the exception of the small control gondola. The dining room extended over two floors and had a surrounding gallery. There were promenade decks with large windows and passenger cabins with one to three beds. In July 1930 the ship took off for Canada with forty-four persons on board and completed the round trip in twenty-five hours. R 100 displayed a number of serious shortcomings, however, and was soon taken out of service. At higher speeds and in rain problems arose with the fluttering shell and the engines also caused problems – problems that could have been fixed, for R 100 "demonstrated capabilities and did not deserve its fate of being grounded after ten successful flights."[24]

R 101 – A Bad Design?

R 101 was fiercely and justifiably criticized even while under construction. It achieved a length of 238.5 meters, a diameter of 40.5 meters and a maximum volume of 156,000m³. Five engines produced 2,924 HP (2,150 kW). There was no ring bracing. R 101 achieved its rigidity solely through massive triangular bearers with cross-section side lengths of three meters and more, which were heavy and took up a lot of space. The passenger areas were generously proportioned like those of R 100, and consequently just fifty-two passengers could be accommodated. And even more weight had to be saved. Kleinheins: "The most important of these measures was the most dangerous: they removed the (excellently designed) mesh nets that had held the gas cells in position. As the framework rings were not under tension, the delicate cells, made in Cardington of goldbeater's skin, were so free to move about that their upper portions changed the horizontal lines of the ship by up to three meters. This had two negative consequences: first the cell walls rubbed through against the bearers (they tried to address this through the use of cushions) and second the ship's stability about its lateral axis worsened considerably. For example, if the nose lifted, because of the lift all of the cells flooded forwards, which enhanced the ship's tendency to rear up. The elevator steersman was forced to constantly make control corrections; steady horizontal flight was thus almost impossible. The shell material was not tear proof, and tears up to forty meters long occurred. ... It was especially bad that the new ... combined maneuvering and overpressure valves opened independently at a pitch of just 3°, causing the ship to lose gas steadily if it porpoised. Consequently R 101 returned from many test flights heavier than when it took off. The dogged adherence to guidelines born of safety requirements and statistics theory, the overloading with innovations, turned a well-conceived ship into a design gone wrong: the seed of destruction had been planted."[25]

Although efforts were made to address its shortcomings through modifications prior to a demonstration flight to Egypt, a sixteen-hour test flight on 1 October 1930 brought no better results. The decision to go ahead with the planned flight despite this was irresponsible; even a well-prepared ship would have had limited chances of survival on such a long flight if it ran into difficulties en route. Kleinheins described the ship's final flight and the end: "One engine failed because of a defect in the cooling system; gas loss resulted in a loss of lift of almost one ton per hour; the undulating and swinging of the gas cells made maintaining a constant altitude without pitching almost impossible. As well, the ship hadn't been flown in bad weather or at maximum speed after the modifications. The new statics report had not yet been completed. Nevertheless, Lord Thompson ordered the ship to take off for Egypt and India on the evening of 4 October 1930. He had announced that it would arrive in India on 13 October, and for political and personal reasons he did not want to deviate. The ship took off in less than ideal weather at 18:30 on 4 October ... with fifty-four persons on board. Among them were some of the leading airship experts in England. ... The rain-heavy ship moved slowly across the Channel. Soon an engine failed; it was repaired. After 7½ hours and 350 kilometers the ship arrived over Beauvais in northern France. At 02:10 on 5 October 1930, the ship, which had become nose-heavy and was at a height of 300 meters, suddenly began to descend. The crew stopped the descent but then it dropped again and struck the hills, not particularly hard. The airship immediately caught fire. Just six members of the crew were rescued from the inferno."[26] This was the end of the German-inspired airship in England. R 100, the last remaining airship, was scrapped.

Airship Hangars and Landing Masts

Large airships required huge open spaces for takeoff and landing. They could not spend extended periods in the open and absolutely needed to be housed in a hangar. This fact was almost always overlooked when new airships were designed, some with gigantic dimensions. Even the smallest Zeppelin, LZ 1, which would have fit almost eighteen times in LZ 129 *Hindenburg*, could not have been built or serviced without a hangar. Even moderate winds found sufficient contact surface on the huge, gas-filled, almost weightless body of an airship to cause difficulties. Temperature fluctuations, which heated or cooled the gas, making the airship lighter or heavier, and rain, which stressed it, were usually more of a problem in the open on the ground than in the air.

It Began with Tents and Wooden Hangars

Early airship hangars were tents and wooden structures which were supposed to offer some protection for the vulnerable airships. The floating hangar on Lake Constance, a simple and all in all practical stopgap solution of the beginning period, has already been described. In the long run, however, it was not usable, for the almost constantly moving surface of the water hampered assembly and maintenance work. The Luftschiffbau Zeppelin's first land hangar in Manzell was an interim solution. It was 126 meters long, 20.85 meters wide and 18.9 meters high. Its closed end was on land and it extended about fifty meters into the lake, where it rested on pilings. As with the floating hangar, the airship rested on a raft, for which they dug a canal beneath the hangar on land. The raft, with airship and handling crew, was pulled out of the hangar by a steamship. The advantages over the floating hangar were minimal.

It had been discovered that, in the long run, the operation of airships was only possible on solid ground, therefore the designing of stationary hangars was begun early on. In many respects they broke new architectural ground. On the one hand there were the huge dimensions, but on the other – and this was the important point – there was the cantilever design with spans that exceeded anything previously imagined. The object was not to build a structure like a church or concert hall, instead the demand was for light structures that were cost-effective and sturdy and could be built with the minimum expenditure of time and materials. For architects and structural engineers, building hangars was a challenge. Building a flyable airship was only slightly less challenging than spanning fifty, even 100 meters without supports and erecting a stable building with a length of 200 or even more than 300 meters.

Hangars for Large Airships

In 1908 the company Brückenbau Flender AG of Benrath won a competition written by the Luftschiffbau Zeppelin GmbH for an airship hangar. It was to have sufficient space, "... for the assembly of two large-type airships side by side, in such a way that work can proceed on each airship without mutual interference."[1] The hangar was 200 meters long, forty-five meters wide and had a clearance of twenty meters. The conditions specified by LZ included the minimum possible temperature deviations in the interior, venting of gas that escaped during filling, lighting, access to the ships, and unimpeded entry and exit by the ships. The last requirement was the most difficult for the Fender AG to meet, for no door had yet been made for an area of 20x43 meters. The company proposed five movable curtains on

The Luftschiffbau Zeppelin's wooden airship hangar in 1906. Half of the hangar was on land, the other half in the water of Lake Constance. Inside the hangar is LZ 3.

Tent hangar with LZ 3 on the Luftschiffbau Zeppelin factory grounds in 1909 (below).

each side that found favor with the judges but were then not adopted, because the required corner towers would have been in the way of a later additional hangar. They therefore decided on a swing gate, whose two wings each consisted of a sliding part and a rotating part.[2] But the problem of the large one-piece door wings had been solved, as demonstrated, for example, by the hangar in Baden-Oos[3] and the double hangar in Potsdam.[4] Numerous proposals were made that were supposed to replace the extremely heavy gates. One was the "folding door," which was submitted to the Luftschiffbau Zeppelin competition by the Sauce & Kloss Company of Berlin. It was unsuccessful. The Italian government did, however, hire the company to build a hangar with folding doors on both ends.[5]

The main problem was the ability to withstand wind. Heavy turbulence often developed at the ends of the hangar. This could pose a danger to airships entering or leaving the hangar, therefore modern hangars received specially-formed end caps that also served as doors.

In 1929 the Goodyear-Zeppelin Corporation constructed a hangar in Akron, Ohio that was distinctive on account of its shape and its huge size. It was 358 meters long, 99 meters wide and 64.5 meters high. At the same time, the Zeppelin-Hallenbau GmbH Berlin erected an airship hangar in Friedrichshafen that had a clear length of 248.5 meters, a clear width of fifty meters and a clear height of forty-six meters. R. Bernhard compared the two structures in detail: "... Despite its smaller size] with a total of 2,200 tons of steel and 150kg per square meter of surface area, the German hangar has just 3.25kg per square meter of converted space, whereas the American hangar, with a total of 7,400 tons of steel and 220kg per square meter, results in 5.7kg per square meter of converted space. The hangar in Friedrichshafen consists of individual double-walled three-joint trusses at ten-meter intervals. ... The foot joints are about 4.5 meters above the ground. The bridge system including wind bracing emerges from [the illustration]. The iron framework of the walls is half-bricked; the superimposed, horizontal lattice girders serve both to support the posts and to prevent the inner truss belt from buckling. The hangar ends are closed by semicircular doors, which slide on a semicircular crane rail next to the hangar ... The roofing consists of 8cm thick lightweight concrete panels, interrupted by putty-free skylights, the side walls of 12cm thick hollow slabs and putty-glazed windows..."[6] The hangar in Akron was sized to accommodate two of the latest type airships, meaning the ZRS 4

Revolving hangar at the naval airship base in Nordholz, summer 1915. The hangar was capable of accommodating two airships. In the background are two conventional airship hangars.

Topping up LZ 127 Graf Zeppelin at the mast in Los Angeles during its round-the-world flight in 1929. The airship is in a state of suspension.

Landing at the mast in Berlin. The anchoring cone is clearly visible on the ship. It was pulled to the mast and then locked vertically downwards into it, but remained free to turn.

Akron and the ZRS 5 *Macon*, simultaneously. Bernhard: "As a result of extensive trials with models, mainly concerning the suction effect caused by wind flow, it has a semi-parabolic cross-section. ... The eleven trusses, spaced at twenty-four meters, are also designed as three-joint trussed girders, but with carriage strap. The carriage strap lies beneath the hangar floor. ... The exterior is entirely sheet metal, of which an approximately thirty meter wide strip of roof is insulated with tarred and graveled roofing paper ... The relatively small skylights are notable. The Americans believe that all work in the hangar must be carried out in artificial light, as the huge body of the airship blocks most natural light." About the doors of the hangar in Akron, Bernhard wrote: "The doors at the ends of the hangar are remarkable. ... They consist of two orange-peel-shaped halves, which are each guided by a bolt (43cm in diameter, 1.38m long) at the top and ride on forty-three wheels at the bottom. These wheels have a diameter of 69cm, are arranged in pairs and run on two appropriately curved tracks. The doors are opened and closed by a 125-HP engine at each end of the hangar via a transmission and rack and pinion drive."[7] Both hangars were equipped with crane tracks, work platforms and various supply installations. Karl Arnstein, a former member of the Friedrichshafen airship company, played a major role in the development of the American hangar. The hangar built on the grounds of Zeppelin's Friedrichshafen facility, was built primarily to accommodate the new large airships, the first of which was LZ 129 *Hindenburg*. Another hangar was built in Löwenthal near Friedrichshafen in 1930-31. Intended for commercial use, it was somewhat larger than the one described above: clear length 270m, width 50m, height 49m. The sidewalls were plastered. The external dimensions were 275m long, 58.4m wide and 53.4m high.[8] Like a construction hangar, the "flight hangar" was also equipped with all the facilities for repair work, such as work platforms, crane trolleys, airship bearers, etc., and could thus also have served as a construction hangar.[9]

Claude Dornier's Rotating Hangars

The rotating hangar is mentioned as a special form, with which Claude Dornier was involved during his early years with LZ. Manfred Bauer wrote: "On behalf of Graf Zeppelin, in 1912 Claude Dornier entered a competition by the Royal Prussian War Ministry for the best solution for a rotating airship Hangar. As Claude Dornier wrote, he was originally given the task of finding out what possibilities there were 'for reinforcing the spider-web-like structure of the framework', in order to safely manage moving the airship in and out of the hangar in strong winds. In such hours it became increasingly clear to me that this goal could never be reached and that only a rotating hangar would make it possible to safely move the airship into

Three airship hangars on the grounds of the Friedrichshafen factory in 1928 with the shadow of LZ 127 Graf Zeppelin. On the right the double hangar of 1909. In 1929 it and the separate hangar next to it built in 1915 were torn down to make way for a new hangar (on right side of photo above). On the left is the airship hangar built in 1916.

and out of the hangar. One evening I was again sitting in the tail of the airship. The last rays of the sun shone through the tall windows of the hangar doors into the large, silent space. As in a vision, I suddenly saw the walls of the hangar rise from the ground. The 'floorless hangar' was born. The idea of building a permanent hangar floor with all the installations, and only rotating the airship's protective housing as it were, proved to be uncommonly productive."[10] Claude Dornier's design won the competition, which was endowed with 80,000 Gold Marks for the winner. In 1912 LZ and Claude Dornier were awarded a patent for a "rotating long hangar for airships." Bauer continued: "In this design the center section ... was designed as a revolving tower, on which the side walls were hung. ... The most significant feature was the

The airship hangars on the grounds of the Friedrichshafen factory in 1936; a low ring-construction hall (not in photo) was later built on the left, next to the left hangar. In it framework rings were assembled lying flat on the floor.

absence of a rotating floor. Previous rotating hangars had a floor that moved with the hangar, which had disadvantages, for example compensating for height differences, etc. In this design the 'hangar floor' was fixed in position based on the local prevailing winds, and when at rest the hangar rested on this fixed base."[11] The four corners of the rotating hangar rested on carriages, which rolled on a circular track. The side parts ran on similar circular tracks, whose center point was the rotation axis of the hangar. A famous example of one such rotating hangar was the double hangar built by the navy in Nordholz during the First World War.

Mobile landing mast in Friedrichshafen-Löwenthal.

The short mast, which was telescopic and mobile, was an ideal mast design. Seen here is the mast in Lakehurst (also see photo on pages 94-95).

The Airship Hangar and the Environment

The hangars were not just constructed as functional buildings. Environmental questions were not as concisely formulated as today, but there was already an awareness that, not least because of the huge scale of the airship hangars, certain aesthetic requirements had to be met. The building of a hangar as the central point of a huge airship base always hewed out a section of nature. And so the engineers strove to minimize the damage. "With their size dominating the surrounding area, airship hangars usually become a new landmark of the cities near which they are built," wrote the VDI magazine in 1913. "They must therefore not only be functional, but also effective in their external appearance. It has been shown that by economically exploiting the existing conditions, and in so doing allowing the suitably chosen construction materials to speak for themselves, it is possible to create structures, even without so-called architectural additions, which are capable of satisfying the beholder."[12]

Landing at the Mast

The landing mast was an additional aid that resulted from experimentation and achieved a satisfactory level of perfection during the period of the last large airships. Nevertheless, the period in the open on the ground at the mast was always associated with danger to the airship. A combination of a low mast with the hangar was ideal.

The so-called tall mast, which was initially used by English and later also by American airships, did not prove itself in the long run. When connected to it, the airship swung freely in the air. A crew had to be on board at all times. As in flight, the trim had to be monitored constantly to keep the ship level. In America, experiments were also made with anchoring at a tall mast on a ship, which was only possible in calm seas, however.[13] How easily an airship anchored on a tall mast could get out of control is illustrated by an incident in 1927, when ZR 3 *Los Angeles* was caught from the rear by an unexpected squall. Its tail was forced upwards until the ship was almost vertical.[14] ZR 3, which had been designed as

ZR 3 Los Angeles standing on its nose at the tall mast in Lakehurst, 1927.

an experimental ship and was extremely robust, survived the incident undamaged. Probably no other ship would have survived as well. In any case it was cause enough for the Americans to abandon the tall mast.[15] The tall mast had other disadvantages. While supplying the ship with lifting gas and fuel exclusively via the mast was useful, all other goods needed to supply the ship plus passengers and crew could only be brought on board by means of it, while the loading of bulky goods was impossible or at least very time-consuming.

Ultimately the short mast, with which the airship was practically resting on the ground, prevailed. A standardized pivoting anchoring cone was attached to the nose of the airship. As with the tall mast, it engaged a funnel on the mast tip and locked there, but remained free to turn. The groundcrew initially used the handling ropes to maneuver the airship near the mast into the wind. A steel cable was lowered from the airship through the anchoring cone. It was fed through the funnel on the mast tip to a winch on the ground, which pulled the ship down until the cone locked into the funnel. The mast had to be telescopic to accommodate different diameter airships. Ideally it was movable and travelled on rails in the axis of the hangar. Outside the hangar there was a circular track with a carriage, to which the tail of the airship was attached, so that the ship could move freely on the anchor mast and turn into the wind. Attached to the anchor mast and tail carriage, the airship could be moved into the hangar. Tracks on either side of the airship with several trolleys provided additional support when the ship was being moved into or out of the hangar.[16]

Size and Performance Comparison of all Zeppelin Airships

The Zeppelin airships completed between 1900 and 1938 were built in twenty-seven different versions (Types a-z, two unknown). The last to be built were twice as long as the first with three-and-a-half times the diameter, with a resulting volume almost twenty times as great. The airships LZ 115-119, LZ 122-125 and LZ 128 were not built, LZ 70 was not completed. In the tables "D"

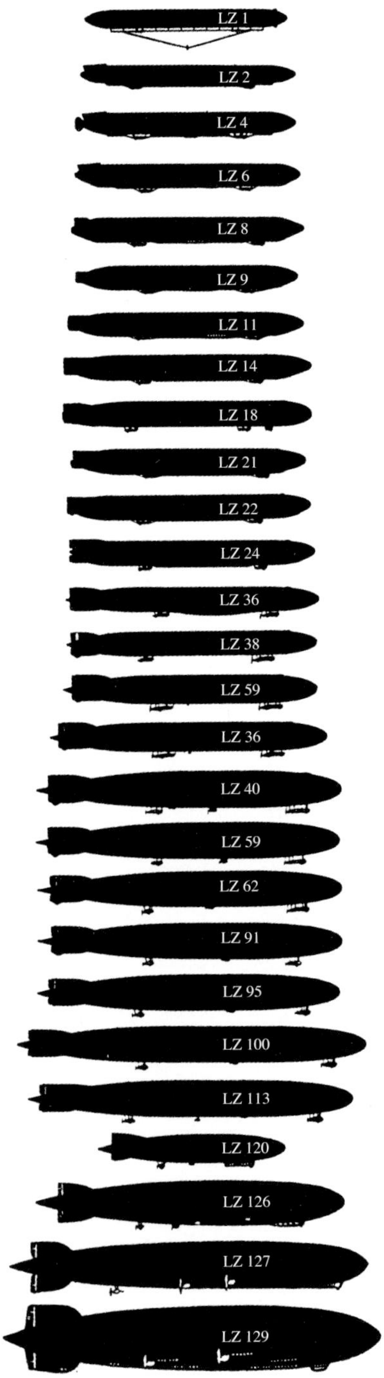

Type	Number	Construction Completed	Length [m]
a	LZ 1	1900	128
b	LZ 2, 3	1905, 1906	128
c	LZ 4, 5	1908, 1909	136
d	LZ 6	1909	136
e	LZ 7, 8	1910, 1911	148
f	LZ 9, 10, 12	1911-1912	140
g	LZ 11, 13	1912-1913	148
h	LZ 14-17, 19, 20	1912-1913	140-15
i	LZ 18	1913	158
k	LZ 21	1913	148
l	LZ 22, 23	1914	156
m	LZ 24, 25, 27-35, 37	1914-1915	158
n	LZ 26	1914	161.2
o	LZ 36, 37	1915	161.4
p	LZ 38, 40-58, 60, 63	1915-1916	163.5
q	LZ 59, 61, 64-71, 73, 77, 81	1915-1916	178.5
r	LZ 62, 72, 74-76, 78-80, 82-90	1916-1917	198
s	LZ 91, 92	1917	196.5
t	LZ 93, 94	1917	196.5
u	LZ 95-99	1017	196.5
v	LZ 100, 101, 103, 105-111	1917-1918	196.5
w	LZ 102, 104	1917	226.5
x	LZ 112-114	1918	211.5
y	LZ 120 (121)	1919	120 (1
z	LZ 126	1924	200
	LZ 127	1928	236.6
	LZ 129, 130	1936, 1938	245

means Daimler and "M" Maybach; total kW is given (total HP). Changes in dimensions caused by subsequent modifications to individual airships are not given if they were from a model series of several ships (for detailed information see Schiller, Hans von: *Zeppelin – Aufbruch ins 20. Jahrhundert*, Bonn 1988).

[m]	**Volume** [m^3]	**Engines** [Number – kW (HP)	**Max. Speed** [kph]	**Range** [km]
11.65	11,300	2D - 21 (28)	—	—
11.65	11,300	2D - 125 (170)	43.9	—
13	15,000	2D - 154 (210)	48.6, 55.8	—
13	15,000	2D - 169 (230)	48.6	2,000
14	19,300	3D - 265 (300)	36	1,600
14	17,800	3M - 320 (435)	75.6	1,600
14	18,700	3M - 375 (510)	80	1,100
14,86	19,550-22,465	3M - 364 (495) – 375 (510)	73.8 – 87.5	2,700
16.6	27,000	4M - 529 (720)	75.6	2,100
14.86	20,870	3M - 397 (540)	73.8	1,900
14.86	22,140	3M - 397 (540)	72	1,900
14.86	22,470	3M - 463 (630)	80.6	2,200
16	25,000	3M - 463 (630)	81	3,300
16	24,900	3M - 463 (630)	85	2,800
18.71	31,900	(3M) 4M - 617 (840)	96	4,300
18.71	35,800	4M - 706 (960)	95.4	4,900
23.93	55,200	6N - 1058 (14400	103.3	7,400
23.93	55,500	5M - 882 (1200)	99.7	10,400
23.93	35,800	5M - 882 (1200)	104	11,500
23.93	55,800	5M - 882 (1200)	107.6 – 114.5	12.200
23.93	56,000	5M - 882 (1200)	108.7	13,500
23.93	68,500	5M - 882 (1200)	103	16,000
23.93	62,200	7M - 1338 (1820)	131.4	12,000
18.71	20,000 (22,500)	3M - 529 (780)	132.5	2,000
27.64	70,000	5M - 1470 (2000)	1242.2	8,500
30.5	105,000	5M - 1948 (2650)	110.2	12,000
41.2	200,000	4D - 3087 (4200)	131	(12,000)

Endnotes

Introduction

1 Wilhelm II (1859- 1941), German Kaiser 1888-1918.

2 Meyer, H.C.: *Airshipmen, Businessmen and Politics 1890-1940*, Washington/London 1991, p. 51.

3 Kleinheins, P. (Hg.): *Die Großen Zeppeline*, Dusseldorf 1985, p. 16.

4 Dürr, L. : *Fünfundzwanzig Jahre Luftschiffbau*, Berlin 1925.

5 Engberding, (D.) : *Luftschiff und Luftschiffahrt in Vergangenheit, Gegenwart und Zukunft*, Berlin 1926.

6 Dörr, W.E.: *Das Zeppelin-Luftschiff "LZ 130,"* in ZVDI, Vol. 82, No. 45, 1938

7 Dörr, W.E.: *Das Zeppelin-Luftschiff "LZ 130,"* in ZVDI, Vol. 82, No. 45, 1938

8 Parseval, A. von: *Graf Zeppelin und die deutsche Luftfahrt*, Berlin undated [1926].

9 Colsman, A.: *Luftschiff voraus! Arbeit und Erleben am Werke Zeppelins*, Stuttgart 1933.

10 Eckener, H.: *Graf Zeppelin: Sein Leben nach eigenen Aufzeichnungen und Erinnerungen*, Stuttgart 1938.

11 Schiller, H. von: Zeppelin – *Wegbereiter des Weltluftverkehrs*, Bad Godesberg 1961.

12 Schiller, H. von: Zeppelin – *Aufbruch ins 20. Jahrhundert*, Bonn 1988

13 Warneken, B.J.: *Zeppelinkult und Arbeiterbewegung* in: *Zeitschrift für Volkskunde*, 80th Vol., 1984/1, p. 59-80.

14 Schmolze, M.: *In der Schwebe. Friedrichshafens Andenken an Zeppelin* in: *Allmende*, 21/22, 1989.

15 Kuhn, E.L.: *Industrialisierung in Oberschwaben und am Bodensee. Geschichte am See* 24/1, 24/2, 2 Vols., Friedrichshafen 1986.

16 Kuhn, E.L.: *Friedrichshafen in der Weimarer Republik*, Friedrichshafen 1986.

17 Burger, O.: *Zeppelin und die Rüstungsindustrie am Bodensee, Teil 1. u. 2.* in: *1999 Zeitschrift für Sozialgeschichte des 20. und 21. Jahrhunderts*. 2nd Vol., Jan. 1987, Issue 1, pp. 8-49 and April 1987, Issue 2, pp. 52-87.

18 Clausberg, K.: Zeppelin. *Die Geschichte eines unwahrscheinlichen Erfolges*, Munich 1979, p. 28.

19 Meyer: *Airshipmen*.

20 see Graf Zeppelin about his work, in: *Zeppelin und Reichskanzler*, handwritten, not dated [1916]. p. 4' "not intended for publication." According to foreword: "[…] Report on a Zeppelin collection in the Prussian House of Representatives […]."

21 Knäusel, H.G.: *Sackgasse am Himmel, Anmerkungen zur Luftschiffahrt damals und heute*, Bonn, 1988.

22 Clausberg: *Zeppelin*, p. 161.

A Cavalry General Becomes a Builder of Airships

1 Vömel, A.: *Graf Ferdinand von Zeppelin – en Mann der Tat*, Emishofen/Konstanz 1908. – Fischer, J.L.: *Der junge Zeppelin* in: Hildebrandt, H. (Hg.): *Zeppelin-Denkmal für das deutsche Volk*, Stuttgart not dated [1925] pp. 1-54. – Rosenkranz, H.: *Ferdinand Graf von Zeppelin. Die Geschichte eines abenteuerlichen Lebens*, Berlin 1931. – Eckener, H. *Graf Zeppelin. Sein Leben nach eigenen Aufzeichnungen und Erinnerungen*, Stuttgart 1938, -- Italiaander, R.: *Graf Ferdinand von Zeppelin. Reitergeneral – Diplomat – Luftschiffpionier*, Konstanz 1980.

2 Engelsing, T. (publisher): *Geliebter Ferdi, schreibe mir sobald Du kannst*, Konstanz 1988.

3 Endres, F.C.: *Vom Kriegsschuler zum General. 1. Militärische Jungend und amerikanischer Krieg*, in: Hildebrandt: *Zeppelin-Denkmal*, pp. 67-82

4 Gilman, R.R.: *Zeppelin in Minnesota. A Study in Fact and Fable*. In: *Minnesota History*, Vol. 39/1965/No. 7, pp. 278-285.

5 (Dincklage F.v.:) *Der Rekognoszierungsritt des Grafen Zeppelin*, Berlin undated.: Endres: *Vom Kriegsschuler […], 3. Im deutsch-französischen Krieg*, in: Hillebrand: *Denkmal*, pp. 90-108.

6 Schnell, K.: *Zeppelins Fernpatrouille mid badischen Dragonern in das Elsass Juli 1870*, Munich 1984.

7 Herzfeldt, R.: *Geschäft und Aufgabe*, Wiesbaden undated [1965]. P. 31.

8 ibid.

9 Heinrich von Stephan (1831-1897), became Postal Inspector-General of the North German League in1870, 1876 Postmaster General of the German Empire; he also organized postal services for other German states, encouraged the formation of the World Postal Association in 1874, invented and introduced the postcard.

10 Johann Heinrich Karl Schütte (1873-1940), Prof. Dr.-Ing. E.h.; naval architect, airship designer.

11 Schütte, J. (publisher): *Der Luftschiffbau Schütte-Lanz (1909-1925)*, Munich/Berlin 1926, p. 1.

12 Zeppelin, Graf von : *Über Zeppelin-Luftschiffe*. Speech to the Society of Naval Architects and Marine Engineers, Stuttgart 27/5/1914 ; Springer, Berlin undated [1914], p. 3.

13 The Papers of Graf Zeppelin (privately owned) see: Terveen, F.: *Über die Anfänge des Zeppelin-Luftschiffs*, in: *Zeppelin-Luftschiffe 1906-1910*, Institut für den wissenschaftlichen Film (publisher), Göttingen 1958, p. 13; Schiller, H.v. *Zeppelin – Wegbereiter des Weltluftverkehrs*, Bonn 1966, p. 19 and p. 25, by same author: *Zeppelin – Aufbruch ins 20. Jahrhundert*, Bad Godesberg 1988, p. 14 and p. 20; Knäusel, H.G.: *LZ 1 – Der erste Zeppelin* (working title, in preparation), Bonn 2000, Chapter 3, Note 1.

14 Clausberg: *Zeppelin*.

15 Zedlitz-Trützschler, R.v.: *Zwölf Jahre am deutschen Kaiserhof*, Stuttgart[5] 1925, p. 197.

16 see Knäusel, H.G.: *Schwarzer Adlerorden für Graf Zeppelin. Zur Geschichte der Luftfahrt im Vorfeld des Ersten Weltkrieges*, in: *Südkurier*, Konstanz, 8/7/1988. Der Schwarze Adlerorden (Order of the Black Eagle), created by King Frederick in 1701, was the highest decoration Prussia had to give.

17 Examples, among others, in: Saager, A. (publisher): *Zeppelin – Der Mensch, der Kämpfer, der Sieger*, Stuttgart undated; Clausberg, K.: *Zeppelin*; Knäusel H.G.: *Zeppelin und Zeppelinismus*, in: *Magazin TRANS*, Berlin 1989, No. 1, p. 13.

18 Knäusel, H.G.: *LZ 1 – Der erste Zeppelin*, Bonn 1985, p. 13.

19 The military airship *La France* made the first guided flight in France in1884.

20 Eckener, H.: *Graf Zeppelin. Sein Leben nach eigenen Aufzeichnungen und Erinnerungen*, Stuttgart 1938, p. 106 ff.

21 ibid: p. 107.

History of the Zeppelin Company

1 Eckener: *Graf Zeppelin*, p. 134.

2 Württemberg District Association: meeting of 6 February 1898, in: ZVDI, Vol. XXXX, No. 15, 11/4/1896, pp. 408-413.

3 The board of directors of the Association of German Engineers: appeal, Berlin, 30/12/1896.

4 Knäusel, H.G.: *LZ 1*, p. 180.

5 ibid, p. 181.

6 ibid, p. 221.

7 Alfred Colsman (1873-1955), director and managing director of the Luftschiffbau Zeppelin GmbH, co-founder of the DELAG and other Zeppelin companies; see Knäusel, H.G.: *Unternehmen Zeppelin*, Bonn 1994, p. 68 ff.

8 Carl Berg (1851-1906), industrialist; first in Germany to manufacture aluminum, was awarded a number of patents for aluminum alloys.

9 Knäusel: *LZ 1*, p. 221 ff.

10 Knäusel: *Unternehmen*, p. 66.

11 Karl Maybach (1879-1960), industrialist, co-founder and technical director of the Luftfahrzeug-Motoren GmbH (later Maybach-Motorenbau GmbH) until 1952.

12 Wilhelm Maybach (1845-1929), industrialist; 1895-1909 technical director of the Daimler-Motoren-Ges. Stuttgart, invented the gas carburetor; co-founder of the Luftfahrzeug-Motoren GmbH.

13 For designations of airships, their technical peculiarities, important flights and their fates, see the next chapter.

14 Knäusel: *Unternehmen*, p. 68.

15 Tittel, L.: *LZ 129 Hindenburg*, Friedrichshafen 1987, p. 30.

16 The name is attributed to the work of the gold-beater, who processed the precious metal into wafer-thin gold leaf, and to do so placed it between delicate skins.

17 Knäusel: *Unternehmen*, p. 69 ff.

18 ibid, see p. 70 ff.

19 Zeppelin, Graf von: *Über Zeppelin-Luftschiffe*. Speech to the Society of Naval Architects and Marine Engineers, Stuttgart 27/5/1914 ; Springer, Berlin undated [1914], p. 10.

20 Knäusel: *Unternehmen*, p. 71.

21 Kuhn, E.L.: *Industrialisierung*, p. 369.

22 ibid

23 ibid., p. 373. Colsman verbatim: "In the turbulent postwar years the leaders of the labor force often reminded me of the count's promise that the houses in the village were to become the property of the workers; after the drastic changes in the value of the houses caused by the war, revolution and inflation, I could not bring myself to fulfill the promise; I also feared that selling might affect the homogeneity of the settlement"; see Colsman: *Luftschiff*, p. 138.

24 Paul Bonatz (1877-1956), professor at the technical institutes in Stuttgart and Istanbul; he erected a number of structures that were advanced for their time, including the main railway station in Stuttgart, the university library in Tübingen and the museum of art in Basel.

25 Sauter, M.: *Die Arbeitersiedlung Zeppelindorf*, in *150 Jahre Ferdinand Graf von Zeppelin*, special edition of the magazine *Baden-Württemberg*, Kalsruhe undated [1988], p. 66 ff.

26 For more information see chapter Airship Hangars and Landing Masts.

27 Claude Dornier (1884-1969), inventor, aircraft designer, entrepreneur, designed rotating airship hangars for the Luftschiffbau Zeppelin GmbH, which were patented beginning in 1912 (patent specification No. 308357). The rotating hangars made it easier to move airships into and out of the hangar in windy conditions.

28 Wachtel, J.: *Claude Dornier – Ein Leben für die Luftfahrt*, Friedrichshafen/Planegg 1989, p. 13 ff ; (all subsequent information on the topic of Dornier is also found there).

29 Alfred Graf von Soden-Fraunhofen (1875-1944), Dipl.-Ing. Dr.Ing. E.h., 1910 head of LZ's experimental department, 1915 technical director of the Zahnradfabrik Friedrichshafen.

30 Meighörner-Schardt, W.: *Alfred Graf von Soden-Fraunhofen. Bilder eines Lebens*, Friedrichshafen 1994, p. 45.

31 Clausberg: *Zeppelin*, p. 70.

32 Herzfeldt: *Geschäft*, p. 94.

33 Knäusel: *Unternehmen*, p. 78.

34 Schiller: *Wegbereiter*, p. 63.

35 ibid

36 Knäusel: *Unternehmen*, p. 78.

37 ibid, pp. 79-80.

38 ibid

39 See Burger: *Zeppelin*, Year 2, Edition 1, p. 22.

40 Colsmann: Luftschiff, p. 207 ff.

41 Hugo Eckener (1868-1954), Dr. Phil., airship captain, from 1924 chairman of the Luftschiffbau Zeppelin GmbH. In the *Frankfurter Zeitung* of 19/10/1900 he said of the second test flight by LZ 1: "[...] the airship [...] floated aptly and prettily over the lake, made small rotations about its vertical axis, perhaps even small turns, [...]. Admittedly [...] there was no real talk of sailing back and forth. [...] And under what conditions were the described modest results achieved? Under the most favorable; there was almost no wind! [...]," according to Italiaander, R.: *Hugo Eckener – Ein moderner Columbus*, Konstanz, 1979, p. 43.

42 Knäusel: *Unternehmen*, p. 79.

43 Knäusel, H.G.: *Zeppelin and the United States of America*, Friedrichshafen 1981.

44 Kuhn: *Weimarer Republik*, p. 37.

45 Hermann Göring (1893-1946), Reich Aviation Minister in 1933, Reichsmarschall in 1940.

46 Wernher Freiherr von Braun (1912-1977), physicist, rocket designer; 1937 director of the Peenemünde Research Station; played a major role in development of the so-called "revenge weapons" V1 and V2 for the Nazis; after 1945 worked on development of rockets in the USA.

47 Burger: *Zeppelin*, Year 2, Edition 2, p. 54 ff.

48 Wilke, O.: *Persönliche Erinnerungen an Graf Zeppelin*, in: Hildebrandt: *Zeppelin-Denkmal*, p. 161.

49 Burger (Note 50) refers here to a speech by Karl Maybach on the occasion of the 25th company anniversary of Maybach-Motorenbau GmbH in 1934, in: ZF (publisher); *Fünfundzwanzig Jahre Zahnradfabrik AG*, Friedrichshafen 1940.

50 Burger: *Zeppelin*, Year 2, Edition 2, p. 52.

51 Hugo Eckener on 10/8/1948, his 80th birthday, to former employees of the Luftschiffbau Zeppelin.

52 Knäusel: *Unternehmen*, p. 98 ff.

The Zeppelin Airships

1 For more information about all relevant early airship projects and studies, see Schmitt, G.: *Vom Ballon zum Luftschiff*, in: Haaland, D, ao.: *Leichter als Luft, Ballone und Luftschiffe*, Bonn 1977, pp. 70-71; and *Vom Luftschiff zur Luftschiffahrt*, in ibid, p. 112-138.

2 Graf Zeppelin's writings (privately owned), usually characterized as diaries, cover the period from his return from the USA in 1863 (according to Terveen, see below) until his death in 1917. Airship captain Hans von Schiller produced copies of several pages. This entry is taken from Schiller's book: *Zeppelin – Wegbereiter des Weltluftverkehrs*, Bonn 1966, p. 19. Also see Terveen, F.: *Über die Anfänge des Zeppelin-Luftschiffs*, in *Zeppelin-Luftschiffe 1906-1910*, Institut für den wissenschaftlichen Film (publisher), Göttingen 1958, p. 12.

3 Even when LZ 1 was already completed and was anything but an air vehicle, Graf Zeppelin still clung to this unusual designation; letter to Rudolf Diesel dated 21/5/1900: "The test flights by my air vehicle are [...]" See Knäusel: *LZ 1*, p. 97.

4 Rudolf von Tschudi (1851-1925), co-founder of the Royal Prussian Airship Battalion, which he commanded as a major from 1891 to 1895.

5 Gottlieb Wilhelm Daimler (1834-1900), inventor and industrialist; was awarded the first patent for a fast-running combustion engine in 1883.

6 Theodor Kober (1865-1930), Dipl.-Ing.; first to undertake design work on the Zeppelin project.

7 August Riedinger (1845-1919), inventor, businessman.

8 Knäusel: *LZ 1*, p. 47.

9 David Schwarz (1850-1897), airship inventor.

10 Rotem, C.: *David Schwarz. Tragödie eines Erfinders*, Bloomington, Indiana, 1983.

11 Schmitt: *Vom Ballon*, pp. 106-111.

12 Carl Berg (1851-1906), businessman, aluminum manufacturer.

13 Berg, C.: *David Schwarz, Carl Berg, Graf Zeppelin*, Munich 1926.

14 Rotem: *David Schwarz*, p. 120 ff.

15 Royal Patent Office, Patent Specification No. 98580, Class 77 Sport; Graf Zeppelin in Stuttgart, steerable airship with several lifting bodies in tandem. Patented in the German Empire on 31 August 1895.

16 Dürr, L.: From construction of the first Graf Zeppelin airship, in: *Werkzeitschrift der Zeppelin-Betriebe*, Year 1 1936, Issue 2, p. 4.

17 Johann Heinrich Karl Schütte (1873-1940) Prof.Dr.Ing.; shipbuilder, airship designer.

18 see Haaland, D.: The Schütte-Lanz airships, in: Haaland, D., *Leichter als Luft*, pp. 196-256.

19 Royal Patent Office, Patent Specification No. 91887, Class 77 Sport; Caesar Eggert in Berlin, balloon of rigid material with flexible inner fabric balloon. Patented in the German Empire on 27 March 1895; see Knäusel: *LZ 1*, p. 54.

20 Berg, C.: *David Schwarz*, p. 42.

21 Ludwig Ferdinand Dürr (1878-1956), Dr.-Ing. E.h.; airship designer; from 1908 technical director of the Luftschiffbau Zeppelin GmbH.

22 Dürr: *Vom Bau*, Zeppelin Company Magazine. Year 1 1936, Issue 2, pp. 4-6, Issue 3, pp. 4-8, Issue 4, pp. 5-6, Year 2 1937, Issue 1, pp. 4-6.

23 Konrad Maximilian Friedrich Maria Baron von Bassus (1874-1928), Dr.phil. h.c.; private scholar, inventor.

24 Hermann W.L. Moedebeck (1857-1910), 1900 Hauptmann in the Royal Prussian Airship Battalion, later Oberstleutnant; publicist.

25 Moedebeck: report on the first test flight by Graf Zeppelin's airship, special issue of *Aeronautische Mitteilungen*, Strasbourg, August 1900.

26 Otto Prince von Bismarck (1815-1899), Reich Chancellor from 1971 to 1890.

27 Hermann von Wissmann (1853-1905), African explorer, Reich commissar, governor of German East Africa 1895-1896.

28 Society for the Promotion of Airship Travel: Report on the first ascent by our air vehicle, 2 July 1900; Friedrichshafen, July 1900, [signed]

Graf Zeppelin.

29 Society for the Promotion of Airship Travel: Report on the second and third ascents by our air vehicle, on 17 and 21 October 1900; Friedrichshafen, July 1900, [signed] Hugo Kübler.

30 Knäusel: *LZ 1*, p. 155.

31 The Order of the Red Eagle, created by King Friedrich in 1791, was Prussia's second-highest decoration after the Order of the Black Eagle. It was awarded in several classes and as a grand cross; see: A Cavalry General Becomes a Builder of Airships, Note 16.

32 August von Parseval (1861-1942), Dr.Ing. E.h., Dr.phil. h.c., airship designer; in the early years he rose to become a serious competitor to Zeppelin with non-rigid designs. Nevertheless he revered Zeppelin and dedicated a biography to him; see Parseval: *Graf Zeppelin*.

33 Nicolaus Basenach (1875-1951), Obering.; together with Hans Gross of the Airship Battalion, he developed a semi-rigid airship system that was adopted by the army.

34 Comment by von Lossow concerning a letter from Zeppelin to the VDI director Albert Lemmer in Brunswick, dated 13/6/1901.

35 Letter of 23/3/1903 from Ludwig Dürr to Zeppelin, on which the latter noted in thick pencil: "Important document for me!" The letter had the following contents (parts not related to the topic of triangular beams omitted):
"[...] To ascertain the rigidity of a triangular girder as proposed by your Excellency, I fabricated a section of such a beam. It consists of three Berg aluminum rods, 2 rods with profile L 20/20/2 and 1 rod with profile 20/20/3. The rods are braced by thin 14/15 mm aluminum tubes. As these are the lightest profiles available, the beam weighs 1.1kg/running meter. This is roughly the same the weight as the lightest 8-meter girder of the earlier 35/25/2, 5 design, with 1.05kg/running meter. Bending stress tests on the earlier beam design revealed that, at loads of 200-250kg/cm^2, the beam so deformed that additional loads would have resulted in complete jack-knifing. (Thus this 200-250kg/cm^2 was not the rigidity of the individual aluminum parts, but of the assembled beam.) The following sketch illustrates the shape of the new beam.

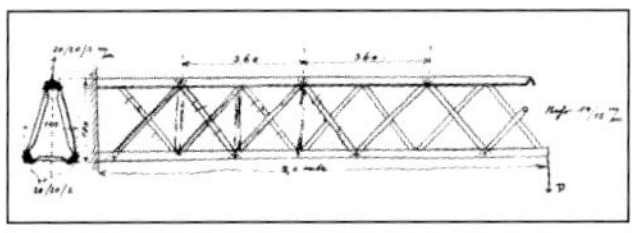

The weight load at P revealed the following: load in kg – downwards bending at P in cm – stress on beam in kg/cm^2 [...]. In reality the downwards bending is not as high as written down, as the restraint (vice) gave way somewhat because of the load. After the stress was removed, the beam displayed no noticeable bending. The rigidity of this arrangement is thus extraordinarily high and the material is approximately three times better used than in earlier designs. Bending resistance in the direction perpendicular to the just-described load, or in the direction of P, is very great. If one rests the two-meter beam on its two ends, it is possible to place a load of 150kg in the center with no permanent bending of the beam. The beam can very easily be attached to a ring of similar construction by riveting an angle onto the ring and then bolting the girder to it, after the ends of the beam were made forked-shape. This will enable construction to proceed much more quickly, for the beam end can be attached securely to the ring by inserting two bolts. By using such beams one could consider using the 18-corner [ring] instead of the 24-corner one. If we brace the adjacent beams in such a way that the tensioning wire or strut goes from the inner side of one beam to the outer side of the other beam and vice versa, the free interior of the balloon will form a 36-corner, almost approaching a circular cylinder, while the exterior retains the 18 corner. The space between the two shells is, however, no longer entirely even throughout, but because of the crosswise tensioning the shells also cannot completely come together. In the 36 corner an inner net is, of course, less necessary than in the 24 corner and could be eliminated completely through the use of an appropriate number of wires or bands. [...]"
Zeppelin's note in pencil at the end of the letter, which deals with weight saving and the possible size of an airship plus the resulting radius of action, is not entirely readable.

36 Meighörner-Schardt, W.: *...der Welt die Wundergabe der Beherrschung des Luftmeeres schenken*, Friedrichshafen 1991, p. 7.

37 Karl Wilhelm von Engen, née von Rothmaler (1853-1934), Prussian general, War Minister 1903-1909.

38 Military Historical Research Institute [publisher]; *Die Militärluftfahrt bis zum Beginn des Weltkrieges 1914*, 3 Volumes, Frankfurt 1965-66, appendix volume. Direct report by the Reich chancellor to the Kaiser concerning measures to promote the Zeppelin project, p/ 57.

39 Military Historical Research Institute [publisher]; *Die Militärluftfahrt*, appendix volume. The Inspectorate of Transportation Units to the General War Department, p. 59. The inspectorate had been established on 1/4/1889; its area of responsibility included all army transportation units, including the entire field of aviation.

40 Zeppelin, Graf: *Die Mainzer Fernfahrt und das Unglück von Echterdingen*, in: Bröckelmann (publisher): *Wir Luftschiffer*, Berlin/Vienna 1909, pp. 307-311.

41 Military Historical Research Institute [publisher]; *Die Militärluftfahrt*, appendix volume, p. 65.

42 Tittel, L.: *Die Fahrten von LZ 4, 1908*, Friedrichshafen 1983, p. 70.

43 Tittel, L.: *Die Fahrten von LZ 4, 1908*, Friedrichshafen 1983, p. 77.

44 Clausberg: *Zeppelin*, Chapter IX, pp. 105-118.

45 see Gemmingen, M. von: *Nachruf*, in: Hildebrand: *Zeppelin-Denkmal*, p. 246 ff;

honorary doctorates from the universities and technical colleges of Leipzig (faculties of philosophy and law), Dresden and Tübingen, and letters of honorary citizenship from Baden-Baden, Ulm, Dresden, Stuttgart, Munich and Worms are illustrated.

46 Knäusel: *Sackgasse*, p. 25.

47 Maximilian Harden, actually Felix Ernst Wittkowski (1861-1927), publicist, publisher of the magazine *Die Zukunft* (1892-1922); personal acquaintance of Bismarck; initially an annexationist, later (after 1916) became a pacifist.

48 Harden, M.: *Das System Zeppelin*, in: *Die Zukunft*, 1/11/1913.

49 Silberer, V.: *Warnende Stimmen in bezug auf Zeppelin-Ballons*, Vienna 1914. – Collection of publications against Zeppelin's rigid system.

50 Groehler, O.: *Geschichte des Luftkriegs 1910 bis 1970*, Berlin 1975, p. 86.

51 ibid

52 Military Historical Research Institute [publisher]; *Die Militärluftfahrt*, text volume, p. 43.

53 Lehmann, E.A.: *Auf Luftpatrouille und Weltfahrt*, Berlin 1936, p. 59.

54 ibid, p. 175

55 Buttlar, H. von: *Zeppeline gegen England*, Leipzig 1931, p. 41 ff.

56 *Times* of 13/1/1919.

57 Neumann, G.P.: *Die deutschen Luftstreitkräfte im Weltkriege*, Berlin 1920,

58 Military Historical Research Institute [publisher]; *Deutsche Militärgeschichte*, Munich 1983, Chapter V, p. 357.

59 Schmalenbach, P.: *Die deutschen Marineluftschiffe*, Herford 1977.

60 ibid, pp. 68-73.

61 Meighörner-Schardt, W.: *Wegbereiter des Weltluftverkehrs wider Willen*, Friedrichshafen 1992. The manuscript was accepted as a dissertation by the philosophical faculty of the Ludwig-Maximilian University, Munich.

62 Paul von Lettow-Vorbeck (1870-1964), General; in the First World War he commanded the German "defense forces" in German East Africa.

63 Kleinheins, P.: *LZ 120 Bodensee und LZ 121 Nordstern*, Friedrichshafen 1994, p. 7.

64 Paul Jaray (1889-1974), graduate of Mechanical Engineering School I, Vienna; 1912 chief designer of the Flugzeugbau Friedrichshafen GmbH, 1914 aerodynamicist with the Luftschiffbau Zeppelin GmbH.

65 Kleinheins: *LZ 120*, ibid.

66 Umberto Nobile (1885-1978), professor, general, airship designer; in 1926 overflew the North Pole in the semi-rigid airship *Norge*, in 1928 led the ill-fated Polar expedition in the semi-rigid airship *Italia*.

67 Warren Gamaliel Harding (1865-1923), 28th president of the United States; opposed his country's participation in the League of Nations, encouraged the 1921 Washington disarmament conference.

68 Knäusel: *United States*, p. 212 ff.

69 See Kleinheins: LZ 120, p. 23 ff.

70 Calvin Coolidge (1872-1933), 30th president of the United States; pursued a policy of moderate isolationism.

71 Schiller: *Aufbruch*, p. 72.

72 ibid, p. 82.

73 ibid, p 85.

74 Adolf Miethe (1862-1927), physicist, professor at the Berlin-Charlottenburg Technical Institute; inventor in the field of photo technology, including color photography.

75 Fridtjof Nansen (1861-1930), Polar explorer; after the First World War he worked to help prisoners of war and populations suffering from hunger; Nobel Peace Prize in 1922.

76 Arthur Koestler (1905-1983), author; took part in the Arctic expedition as a correspondent for Ullstein, Berlin.

77 Schiller: *Aufbruch*, p. 90.

78 ibid, p. 95 ff.

79 ibid, p. 100.

80 Ratio of length to maximum, diameter.

81 Wilhelm Ernst Dörr (1882-1954), Dipl.-Ing.; 1910 engineer with DELAG, 1915 director of the Luftschiffbau Zeppelin GmbH.

82 Occasional verbatim quotes by Dörr are not marked.

83 According to Dörr: *LZ 129*.

84 Schiller: *Aufbruch*, p. 103 ff.

85 ibid, p. 104.

86 Sammt, A.: *Mein Leben für den Zeppelin*, Wahlwies, undated, p. 127.

87 Franklin Delano Roosevelt (1882-1945), 32nd president of the USA; introduced reforms to combat the world economic crisis (New Deal).

88 Moltmann, G.: *Die Luftschiff Hindenburg Katastrophe und das Heliumproblem*, in: *Wehr-Wissenschaftliche Rundschau*, Year 11, Nov. 1961, pp. 617-634.

89 Bauer, M. and Duggan, J.: *LZ 130 Graf Zeppelin und das Ende der Verkehrsluftschiffahrt*, Friedrichshafen 1994, p. 83.

90 Eckener, H.: *Im Zeppelin über Länder und Meere*, Flensburg 1949, p. 558.

91 Dörr: *LZ 130*.

92 Ballast water scavenging systems were developed prior to the First World War and tested in LZ 13 *Hansa*.

93 Bauer: LZ 130, (Chapter 5), p. 106 ff and ibid (Tables) pp. 204-206.

Attempts to Retrieve the Past

1 Zeppelin Luftschifftechnik GmbH: *Der Zeppelin NT im humanitären Einsatz*, press release, April 2000, No. 5.

2 Zeppelin NT = Zeppelin New Technology.

3 see Hilligardt, E., and Sperger, A. (publisher): *Bericht über die Luftschiffstudie LZ 132*; typescript 3+38 pages, illustrated, Friedrichshafen, 24/6/1957. Extensive drafts concerning the LZ 132 airship study survive in Friedrichshafen; until the 1970s the project was pursued or used as the basis of further development by other groups.

4 A poll revealed that the name Zeppelin had a name recognition of 70% (information from Zeppelin-Luftschifftechnik).

5 Knäusel: *Sackgasse*, p. 62.

6 Hagenlocher, K.G.: *Zurück in die Zukunft*, in: *Spektrum der Wissenschaft*, January 2000, p. 82 ff.
7 Designation for the prototype.
8 Hess, Chr.: *Comeback der Luftschiffe*, in: *Flug Revue*, March 2000, p. 25.
9 ibid, p. 26
10 The technical description of the Zeppelin N 07 is based on its status at the beginning of 2007.

Zeppelin "Relatives"

1 20 October 1917, forced landing after running out of fuel near Bourbonne les Bains in Burgundy; the French military was able to prevent the crew from destroying the airship.
2 Shenandoah, Indian; from Robinson, D.H. and Keller, C.L.: *Up Ship! U.S. Rigid Airships 1919-1935*, Annapolis, Maryland 1982, p. 73 = Daughter of the Stars, but doubtful (see Footnote 10, p. 222).
3 Z stood for Zeppelin and R for rigid.
4 Kleinheins: *Die großen Zeppeline*, p. 120.
5 ibid, p. 200.
6 Robinson : Up Ship !, p. 104 ff.
7 Kleinheins: *Die großen Zeppeline*, p. 201.
8 ibid
9 Karl Arnstein (1887-1975), Dr.Ing. ; airship designer, vice-president of the Goodyear-Zeppelin Corporation. After war broke out in September 1939, the company called itself Goodyear Aircraft Corporation. Arnstein remained with the company until 1959.
10 Smith, R.K.: *The Airships Akron and Macon*, Annapolis, Maryland 1965, p. 45.
11 Ebner, H.: *Das amerikanische Starrluftschiff "Akron,"* in: ZVDI, Vol. 76, No. 2, 9/1/1932, pp. 37-40.
12 The Luftschiffbau Zeppelin in Friedrichshafen also experimented with swiveling propellers but soon abandoned the idea. Because of the placement of the engines in outboard gondolas, a safety requirement for hydrogen airships, swiveling the propellers would have required a technically-complex arrangement.
13 Smith: *Akron and Macon*, pp 77-96. A description and reconstruction of ZRS 4's last flight.
14 Rescue systems were often discussed by airship crews during the war, but as every kilo of additional weight reduced the airship's performance their adoption was deferred. First-aid equipment was also dispensed with, as were life vests, which froze at high altitude and became unusable. The use of parachutes would only have made sense if the crew wore them at all times, but the limited space on board made this impossible. Initially they were attached to the outside of the gondolas but then were completely done away with. As well, a crashing, burning airship would soon have overtaken a crewmember suspended beneath a parachute; see Schmalenbach: *Marineluftschiffe*, p. 68 ff.
15 Smith: *Akron and Macon*, p. 98.
16 Kleinheins: *Die großen Zeppeline*, p. 215.
17 ibid
18 The reader is referred to the extensive English-language literature, including : Higham, R. : *The British Rigid Airship 1908-1931*, London, Southampton 1961; Abbott, P.: *Airship – The Story of R 34 and the first East-West Crossing of the Atlantic by Air*, Bath, Somerset 1973; Hartcup, G.: *The Achievement of the Airship*, Vancouver 1974; Countryman, B.: *R 100 in Canada*, Erin, Ohio 1982; Chamberlain, G.: *Airships*, Cardington, Suffolk 1984.
19 Kleinheins: *Die großen Zeppeline*, p. 118.
20 ibid.
21 ibid, p. 120.
22 ibid.
23 ibid.
24 ibid, p. 186 ff.
25 ibid, p. 191.
26 ibid, p. 208.

Airship Hangars and Landing Masts

1 Luftschiffbau Zeppelin GmbH's airship hangar in Friedrichshafen, built by Brückenbay Flender A.G., in: ZVDI, Vol. 53, No. 31, 31/7/1909, p. 1227 ff.
2 ibid, p. 1229
3 VDI magazine, Vol. 57, No. 18, 3/5/1913, p. 681.
4 ibid, p. 682 ff.
5 VDI magazine, Vol. 55, No. 14, 8/4/1911, p. 569 ff.
6 Bernhard, R.: *Die beiden neuesten Hallen für Zeppelin-Luftschiffe*, in :VDI magazine, Vol. 74, No. 44, 1/11/1930, p. 1512.
7 ibid, p. 1513.
8 Bauer, M.: *Luftschiffhallen in Friedrichshafen*, Friedrichshafen 1985, p. 60 ff.
9 ibid, p. 71.
10 Quoted from: ibid, p. 40.
11 ibid.
12 *Die Luftschiffhalle im Luftschiffhafen zu Potsdam*, in: VDI magazine, Vol. 57, No. 18, p. 681.
13 Robinson : *Up Ship !*, p. 87 ff.
14 ibid, p. 151 ff.
15 ibid, p. 154.
16 Kleinheins: *Die großen Zeppeline*, p. 129 ff.

Bibliography and List of Sources

Abbott, P.: *Airship - The story of R 34 and the first East-West Crossing of the Atlantic by Air*, Bath/Somerset, 1974.

Althoff, W.F.: *Sky Ships - A History of the Airships in the United States Navy*, New York, 1990.

Archbold, R.: *Luftschiff Hindenburg und die große Zeit der Zeppeline*, München, 1994.

Architectural Association, The: *Housing the Airship*, London, 1989.

Bassus, K.v.: *Über das Graf Zeppelin'sche Luftschiff*, Sonderdruck aus: "Bayerisches Industrie- und Gewerbeblatt," München, 1901.

Bauer, M.: *Luftschiffhallen in Friedrichshafen*, Friedrichshafen, 1985.

Bauer, M., u. J. Duggan: *LZ 130 Graf Zeppelin und das Ende der Verkehrsluftschiffahrt*, Friedrichshafen, 1994.

Berg, C.: *David Schwarz - Carl Berg - Graf Zeppelin*, München, 1926; (Nachdruck Verdohl/Eveking 1953).

Bernhard, R.: *Die beiden neuesten Hallen für Zeppelin-Luftschiffe* in: "Zeitschrift des VDI," Bd. 74,1930, Nr.44.

Bröckelmann (Hg.): *Wir Luftschiffer - Die Entwicklung der modernen Luftschifftechnik in Einzeldarstellungen*, Berlin/Wien, 1909.

Burger, O.: *Zeppelin und die Rüstungsindustrie am Bodensee*, in "1999 - Zeitschrift für Sozialgeschichte des 20. und 21. Jahrhunderts," 1987, Hefte 1 und 2.

Buttlar, H. v.: *Zeppeline gegen England*, Leipzig, 1931.

Chamberlain, G.: *Airships - Cardington*, Suffolk, 1984.

Clausberg, K.: *Zeppelin - Die Geschichte eines unwahrscheinlichen Erfolges*, München, 1979.

Colsman, A.: *Luftschiff voraus! Arbeit und Erleben am Werke Zeppelins*, Stuttgart 1933 (Reprint: München, 1983).

Countryman, B.: *R 100 in Canada*, Erin/Ontario, 1982.

Deighton, L.: *Airshipwreck*, London, 1978.

(Dincklage, F.v.:) *Der Rekognoszierungsritt des Grafen Zeppelin*, Berlin, o.J.

Dörr, H. (s. Überlingen).

Dörr, W.E.: *Das Zeppelin-Luftschiff LZ 129*, in: "Zeitschrift des VDI," Bd.80, Nr.13, 1936.

Ders.: *Das Zeppelin-Luftschiff LZ 130*, in: "Zeitschrift des VDI," Bd.82, Nr.45, 1938.

Dürr, L.: *Fünfundzwanzig Jahre Zeppelin-Luftschiffbau*, Berlin, 1925.

Ders.: *Vom Bau des ersten Zeppelin-Luftschiffs*, in: "Werkzeitschrift der Zeppelin-Betriebe," Jg. 1936, Nr.2, 3, 4, Jg. 1937, Nr.1.

Eckener, H.: *Graf Zeppelin - Sein Leben nach eigenen Aufzeichnungen und Erinnerungen*, Stuttgart, 1938.

Ders.: *Im Zeppelin über Länder und Meere*, Flensburg, 1949.

Eichler, J.: *Luftschiffe und Luftschiffahrt*, Berlin, 1993.

Engberding: *Luftschiff und Luftschiffahrt in Vergangenheit, Gegenwart und Zukunft*, Berlin, 1926.

Engelsing, T. (Hg.): "Geliebter Ferdi, schreibe mir sobald Du kannst," Konstanz, 1988.

Gesellschaft zur Förderung der Luftschiffahrt: *Bericht über das Er-gebnis der ersten Auffahrt unseres Luftfahrzeugs, 2. Juli 1900, Friedrichshafen, 1900.*

Dies.: *Bericht über das Ergebnis der zweiten und dritten Auffahrt unseres Flugschiffes am 17. und 21. Oktober, Friedrichshafen 1900.*

Groehler, O.: *Geschichte des Luftkrieges 1910 bis 1970*, Berlin, 1975.

Gilman, R.R.: *Zeppelin in Minnesota - A Study in Fact and Fable*, in: "Minnesota History," Vol.39, Nr.7.

Griehl, M., u.J. Dressei: *Zeppelin! The German Airship Story*, London, 1990.

Gritzner, M.: *Handbuch der Ritter- und Verdienstorden*, Leipzig, 1893 (Reprint 1981).

Haaland, D.: *Der Luftschiffbau Schütte-Lanz Mannheim-Rheinau (1909-1925)*, Mannheim, 1987.

Dies., u.H.G. Knäusel, G. Schmitt, J. Seifert: *Leichter als Luft - Ballone und Luftschiffe* (Reihe: Die deutsche Luftfahrt, Bd. 26), Bonn, 1997.

Harden, M.: *Das System Zeppelin*, in: "Die Zukunft," 1. November 1913.

Hartcup, G.: *The Achievement of the Airship*, Vancouver, 1974.

Herzfeldt, R.: *Geschäft und Aufgabe*, Wiesbaden o.J.

Heuss, Th.: *Erinnerungen 1905-1933*, Tübingen, 1963.

Ders.: *Robert Bosch. Leben und Leistung*, Tübingen, 1946.

Higham, R.: *The Britsh Rigid Airship 1908-1931*, London/Southampton, 1961.

Hildebrandt, H. (Hg.): *Zeppelin-Denkmal für das deutsche Volk*, Stuttgart, o.J.

Hoernes, H. (Hg.): *Buch des Fluges*, Bd. 3, Wien, 1912.

Ingold, F.P.: *Literatur und Aviatik*, Basel/Stuttgart, 1978.

Institut für den wissenschaftlichen Film (Hg.): *Zeppelin-Luftschiffe 1906-1910*, Göttingen, 1958.

Italiaander, R.: *Ferdinand Graf von Zeppelin, Reitergeneral - Diplomat - Luftschiffpionier*, Konstanz, 1980.

Ders.: *Ein Deutscher namens Eckener*, Konstanz, 1981.

Kleinheins, P. (Hg.): *Die großen Zeppeline - Die Geschichte des Luftschiffbaus*, Düsseldorf, 1985.

Ders.: *LZ 120 Bodensee und LZ 121 Nordstern*, Friedrichshafen, 1994.

Knäusel, H.G.: *LZ 1 - Der erste Zeppelin*, Bonn, 1985 (2. Aufl. in Vorb.).

Ders.: *Sackgasse am Himmel*, Bonn, 1988.

Ders.: *Schwarzer Adlerorden für Graf Zeppelin*, in: "Südkurier," Konstanz, 8.7.1988.

Ders.: *Unternehmen Zeppelin - Geschichte eines Konzerns*, Bonn, 1994.

Ders.: *Zeppelin and the United States of America*, Bonn, 1981.

Ders.: *Zeppelin und Zeppelinismus*, in: "Magazin TRANS," Nr.1, Berlin, 1989.

Kuhn, E.L.: *Industrialisierung am Bodensee*, Friedrichshafen, 1984.

Ders.: *Friedrichshafen in der Weimarer Republik*, Friedrichshafen, 1986.

Lehmann, E.A.: *Auf Luftpatrouille und Weltfahrt*, Berlin, 1936.

Meighörner-Schardt, W.: "... der Welt die Wundergabe der Beherrschung des Luftmeeres schenken," Friedrichshafen, 1991.

Ders.: *Wegbereiter des Weltluftverkehrs wider Willen. Die Geschichte des Zeppelin-Luftschifftyps "w,"* Friedrichshafen, 1992.

Ders.: *Alfred Graf von Soden-Fraunhofen*, Friedrichshafen 1994.

Meyer, H.C.: *Airshipmen Businessmen and Politics 1890-1940*, Washington, 1991.

Meyers großes Personenlexikon, Mannheim, 1968.

Meyers Lexikon, Leipzig 1926-1930

Miethe, A., u.H. Hergesell (Hg.): *Mit Zeppelin nach Spitzbergen*, Berlin/Leipzig/Wien/Stuttgart, 1911.

Militärgeschichtliches Forschungsamt (Hg.): *Deutsche Militärgeschichte*, Bd.5, München, 1983.

Dass.: *Die Militärluftfahrt bis zum Beginn des Weltkrieges 1914*, Textbd.u. Anlagebd., Berlin, 1965.

Moedebeck, H.W.C.: *Erster Fahr-Versuch mit dem Luftschiff des Grafen Zeppelin*, Sonderheft "Illustrirte Aeronautische Mittheilungen," Straßburg, August 1900.

Moltmann, G.: *Die Luftschiff-Hindenburg-Katastrophe und das Heliumproblem*, in: "Wehr-Wissenschaftliche Rundschau," 11.Jg., November, 1961.

Neumann, G.P. (Hg.): *Die deutschen Luftstreitkräfte im Weltkriege*, Berlin, 1920.

Parseval, August v.: *Graf Zeppelin und die deutsche Luftfahrt*, Berlin, o.J. [1926],

Patentschriften, Deutsche: Nr.91887, Nr.98580.

Rimell, R.L.: Zeppelin! *A Battle for Air Supremacy in World War I*, London, 1984.

Robinson, D.R., u. C.L. Keller: *Up Ship! - U.S. Rigid Airships 1919-1935*, Annapolis/Maryland, 1982.

Rosenkranz, H.: *Ferdinand Graf von Zeppelin - Die Geschichte eines abenteuerlichen Lebens*, Berlin, 1931.

Rotem, C.: *David Schwarz. Tragödie eines Erfinders*, Bloomington, Indiana 1983.

Saager, A. (Hg.): *Zeppelin - Der Mensch, der Kämpfer, der Sieger*, Stuttgart, o.J.

Sammt, A. (Bearb.: W. v. Zeppelin und P. Kleinheins): *Mein Leben für den Zeppelin*, Wahlwies, o.J.

Sauter, M.: Die Arbeitersiedlung Zeppelindorf, in: *Ferdinand Graf von Zeppelin* (Sonderausgabe der Zeitschrift Baden-Württemberg), Karlsruhe, o.J.

Schiller, H. v.: *Zeppelin - Wegbereiter des Weltluftverkehrs*, Bad Godesberg, 1966.

Ders.: *Zeppelin - Aufbruch ins 20. Jahrhundert*, Bonn, 1988.

Schmalenbach, P.: *Die deutschen Marineluftschiffe*, Herford, 1977.

Schmölze, M.: *In der Schwebe. Friedrichshafens Andenken an Zeppelin*, in: "Allmende," 21/22, 1989.

Schnell, K.: *Zeppelins Fernpatrouille mit badischen Dragonern in das Elsaß Juli 1870*, München, 1984.

Schütte, J. (Hg.): *Der Luftschiffbau Schütte-Lanz 1909-1925*, München/Berlin, 1926.

Schwipps, W.: *Riesenzigarren und fliegende Kisten*, Berlin, 1984.

Silberer, V. (Hg.): *Warnende Stimmen in bezug auf Zeppelin-Ballons*, Wien, 1914.

Smith, R.K.: *The Airships Akron and Macon*, Annapolis, Maryland, 1972.

Strahlmann, F. (Hg.): *Zwei deutsche Luftschiffhäfen des Weltkrieges, Ahlhorn und Wildeshausen*, Oldenburg, i.O., 1926.

Sturm, F.: *Vortriebsanlage des Zeppelin-Luftschiffs LZ 129*, in: ZVDI, Bd. 80, Nr.13, 393ff.

Tittel, L.: *Die Fahrten des LZ 4 1908*, Friedrichshafen, 1983.

Ders.: *LZ 129 Hindenburg*, Friedrichshafen, 1987.

Uberlingen, Stadtverwaltung (Hg.): *Wilhelm Ernst Dörr 1882-1954*, Überlingen, 1993.

(VDI) Württembergischer Bezirksverein: *Sitzung vom 6. Februar 1898*, in: "Zeitschrift VDI," Bd. XXXX, No.15.

Vömel, A.: *Graf Ferdinand von Zeppelin - Ein Mann der Tat*, Emmis-hofen/Konstanz, 1908.

Wachtel, J.: *Claude Dornier - Ein Leben für die Luftfahrt*, Friedrichshafen/Planegg, 1989.

Warneken, B.J.: *Zeppelinkult und Arbeiterbewegung*, in: "Zeitschrift für Volkskunde," 80. Jg., 1984/1.

Zedlitz-Trützschler, R. v.: *Zwölf Jahre am deutschen Kaiserhof*, Stuttgart, 1924.

Zeppelin, F. v.: *Erfahrungen beim Bau von Luftschiffen*, Berlin, 1908.

Ders.: *Die Eroberung der Luft*, Stuttgart/Leipzig, 1908.

Ders.: *Uber Zeppelin-Luftschiffe*, Berlin, o.J.

Ders.: *Graf Zeppelin über sein Werk*, in: "Zeppelin und Reichskanzler," gedr. Handschrift, o.J.

ZVDI: *Die Luftschiffhalle des Luftschiffbau Zeppelin G.m.b.H. in Friedrichshafen*, Bd.53, Nr.31, 31.7.1909.

Dies.: *Die Luftschiffhalle im Luftschiffhafen zu Potsdam*, Bd.57, Nr.18, 3.5.1913.

Dies.: *Luftschiffhalle mit Falttoren*, Bd.55, Nr.14, 8.4.1911.

Dies.: *Entwürfe für lenkbare Luftschiffe* (Vortrag Zeppelin), Bd.XXXX, Nr.15, 11.4.1896.

Index

Abbreviations

DELAG Deutsche Luftschiffahrts AG
DZR Deutsche-Zeppelin-Reederei
FIF Fahrzeuginstandsetzung GmbH Friedrichshafen
ILbA Internationale Luftschiffahrtausstellung (International Airship Travel Exhibition)
L (Number)Zeppelin naval airship; coded designation, number not the same as construction number
LZ Luftschiffbau Zeppelin GmbH
LZ (Number)Construction number for Zeppelin airships; also Zeppelin army airships; however number then not identical to construction number.
R (Number)English airship, Zeppelin system
VDI Verein Deutscher Ingenieure
Z (Number)Zeppelin army airship; number not identical to construction number.
ZEWAS Zeppelin Hydrogen and Oxygen Works GmbH
ZT Gear Factory Friedrichshafen
ZLT Zeppelin Luftschifftechnik GmbH
ZR (Number) and
ZRS (Number)American rigid airship, Zeppelin system
ZVDI Magazine of the Association of German Engineers

Hindenburg